Cemetery Gates

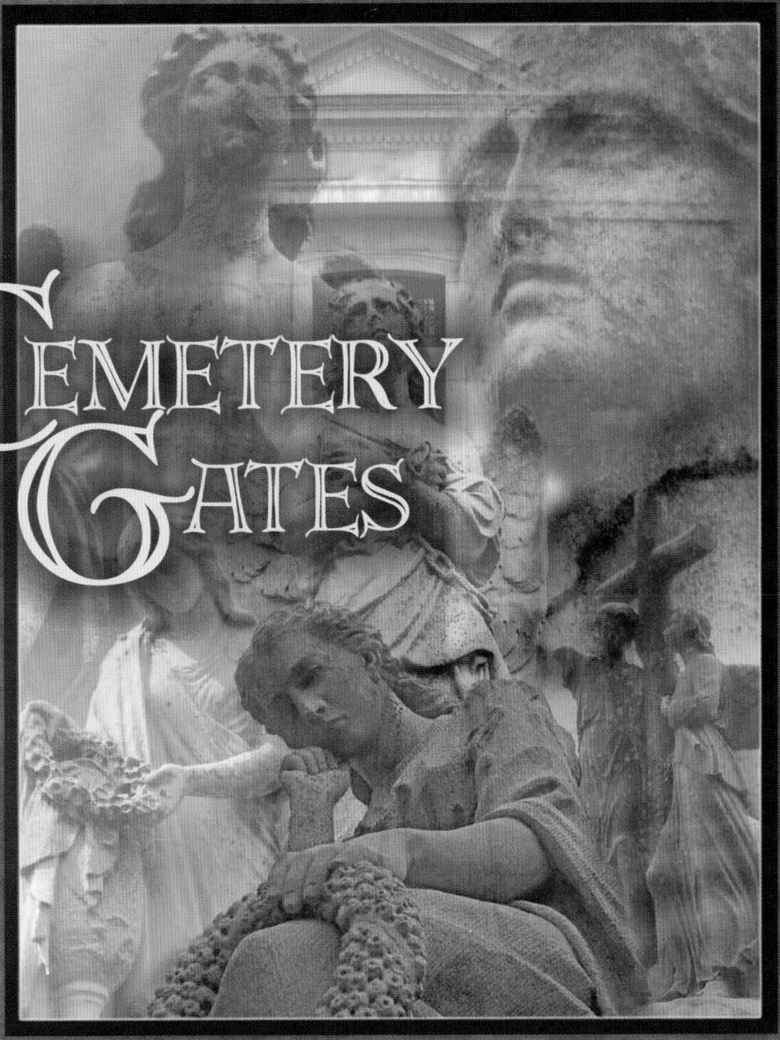

Death and Mourning Through the Ages

Corvis Nocturnum

4880 Lower Valley Road · Atglen, Pennsylvania 19310

Text by author
Images by author unless otherwise noted

Published by Schiffer Publishing Ltd.
4880 Lower Valley Road
Atglen, PA 19310
Phone: (610) 593-1777; Fax: (610) 593-2002
E-mail: Info@schifferbooks.com

In Europe, Schiffer books are distributed by
Bushwood Books
6 Marksbury Ave.
Kew Gardens
Surrey TW9 4JF England
Phone: 44 (0) 20 8392-8585; Fax: 44 (0) 20 8392-9876
E-mail: info@bushwoodbooks.co.uk
Website: www.bushwoodbooks.co.uk

Library of Congress Control Number: 2011927150

Designed by RoS
Type set in DeRoos/Book Antigua

ISBN: 978-0-7643-3787-1

Printed in China

In memory of my family and friends who have passed on, especially to my grandmother, who loved the occult, the paranormal, and all of the creative arts.

And to Starr, Jack, and Michelle for helping me make Dark Moon Press what it has become.

ACKNOWLEDGEMENTS

The author would like to thank the following people for their inspiration, as well as for editing and previewing thoughts: my editor, Dinah Roseberry, Mr. Schiffer, and Reverend Tim Shaw, Michelle Belanger, Katherine Ramsland, Starr, and Raven Digitalis, to name a few. A special thanks to Drake Mefestta, Ticia, Kambriel, Onyx, and Mistress Rea.

Your patience, thoughts, and hours of delightful conversation were instrumental to the completion of this work. However, I enjoy most of all your friendship.

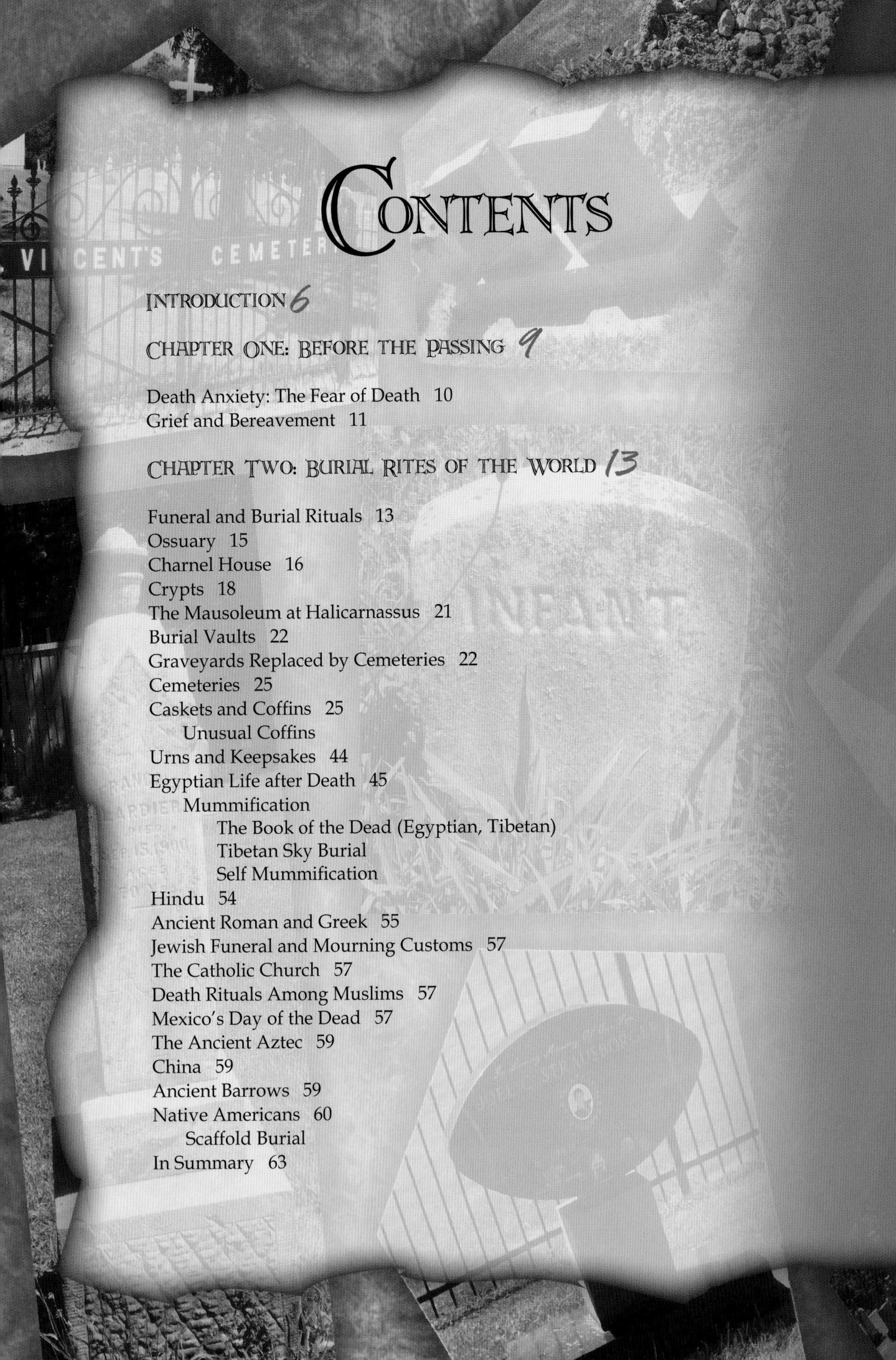

Contents

Introduction

Death is the veil which those who live call life:
They sleep, and it is lifted.

~ Percy Bysshe Shelley

Death. With both fear and fascination, we have all reflected inward, silently wondering about our own demise. Fear of the end, what may (or may not) lay beyond, is what keeps the topic of death a taboo. It is, however, our morbid fascination with understanding, the gathering of knowledge and experience, that drives us ever forward, especially into the subject of our own mortality. *Cemetery Gates: Death and Mourning Through the Ages* will examine death, its significance in religious and ethnic views, cultural myths, and its use in both art and literature throughout the ages. When we examine works from the Romantic era, writers such as Mary Shelley, Lord Byron, and Edgar Allan Poe, we begin to see the underlying tones from which the modern Gothic culture has evolved ... the beauty in the darkness (and death), the withered rose held in high regard, and the decay from whence it grows. One cannot fully appreciate the light ... without first having walked in the darkness.

What people fear, they are also fascinated with, and so *Cemetery Gates: Death and Mourning Through the Ages* attempts to explain how the different religions and ethnic groups understand this inevitable event, the mourning that accompanies it, as well as the significance that people have given death. We'll explore cultural myths and psychological symbolism ascribed to death and dying in art and fiction. Some of these things were created from the very idea that beauty in darkness (and death) was to be appreciated and held in high regard to keep things in proper prospective.

Poetically it has been said that the sands of time wait for no one, and as our last breath escapes our bodies, there are no second chances to go back and do what has been left for later. Our earthly legacy lives on in the memories of others, even as monuments that time and elements slowly erode away. Ironically, on an ancient great stone figure is inscribed the words, "Look upon my wonders mere mortals and despair." Despite its lofty declaration, time will make it completely dust. The one thing that unifies all living things is that they die, which, all the more, gives meaning to life. Anyone's belief in life and an afterlife is going to be influenced by their own feelings and interpretation of the significance of death. This has held true for people as long they have walked the Earth. Due to the beliefs of many people all over, from ancient China and Egypt especially, vast fortunes were set aside by leaders of various cultures as they built structures to house not only their remains but that of possessions and even spouses and servants, even if the spouses and servants were still alive (gruesome as it may seem to our ethics).

The method of preparation for the journey into the next world varies widely from religion to religion. According to the Hindu belief, it is necessary for the skull to be broken by a blow at the cremation ground to free the soul from entrapment within it. Within Islamic countries, a Muslim's body must be washed at least three times after death with soap and water. Perfume may be used, or camphor placed, in the orifices and armpits, while prayers are said followed by passages being read from the *Qur'an.*

Death's impact held greater magnitude in days past due to diseases or war, which could lead to the end of an entire community. As populations increased, the need for structure and order for the whole of the community increased, causing people to choose their own life path within their society. Within these evolving societies, the roles people played became more important than the individual.

The tragic feeling of living as if we are all disposable has become a disturbing and frightening feeling in our modern world, which creates a sense of loss for personal dignity. I would even go so far as to wager that our time here on this Earth has been made to seem almost meaningless – unless of course we as individuals make every effort to stand out, to be remembered for having accomplished something of value in our lives, lest we, by our own choice, make our existence seem almost insignificant. One might say that the individual and their own uniqueness to the world and how we treasure each other seems to go by the wayside while urbanization and modern technology rapidly continue to bring a fundamental shift in the relationship between people. Looking at most of Europe, one can sense things still have an old world air about them. Some sectors of rural America still retain some of the sensibility of values and the need for the individual. People in these places tend to see one another as a person, and they grow old together. In the case of death of one of the community's members in our past, the passing could not be simply ignored because it was felt on an emotional level as well as important to the social hierarchy. Death then became more than a simple disruption; it was felt on a vastly more personal and social level. They ritually marked the passing with funeral services in order to assist both family and friends of the departed in a small but close-knit group in their grieving, to act as a support to process the event and move on together.

In modern times, however, the loss of an individual seems to have become less noticed, as strangers within large cities hardly interact or merely pass each other by without a glance. Relations between people become less and less of a personal bond and more of a cold achievement of similar goals. People have become almost totally irrelevant; we now interact toward most others solely due to the roles that they play, as if we were parts of a large machine where we all exist as pieces of a whole. In this case, grief is usually very limited to the family and friends of the deceased for a mere few days off work before they are expected to return unaffected by a loss felt so deeply.

We as a society become ever increasingly desensitized by death and its accompanying violence. In everything from video games to movies and even in our news we are shown bodies lying on the streets of major cities all over the world. Death counts from accidents, wars, or natural disasters like hurricanes or sweeping fires ever increasingly get shoved into our faces on newscasts. Death has become the subject of films from the *Faces of Death* series depicting real footage of death of people from executions, accidents and animals being killed to *Flatliners* in the 1990s. Television series like *Six Feet Under* (which had a huge following) and *1000 Ways To Die* have become very popular. Humanity appears less caring overall and life passes us by ever faster. As such, it is our responsibility as individuals to appreciate our own lives and loved ones even more, and enrich the world around us.

Chapter One

Before the Passing

"Death is one of two things. Either it is annihilation, and the dead have no consciousness of anything; or, as we are told, it is really a change: a migration of the soul from one place to another."

~ Socrates

The first definition of death in *Webster's Dictionary* is that it is "the act of dying; the end of life; the total and permanent cessation of all the vital functions of an animal or plant." This appears easy enough to comprehend, until we realize that it represents a largely Western conception of death. Some cultures believe that life departs the body of a person in different situations, such as with illness or sleep. As such, people can be said to "die" several times before their final passing. This also means that a person can be defined as dead without meeting many of the criteria found in medical texts.

As people age, they may notice a decline in their health and/or the ability to do certain tasks. To some, this is a realization that the end must be coming and the individual begins to prepare for death and is even viewed as being dead long before our Western perceptions would acknowledge it.

The Hindu envision a circular pattern of life and death where a person is believed to die and be reborn again, repeatedly, in great contrast with the fundamental Christian view where death is believed to occur only once and rebirth is in Heaven. Further removed from that thinking, among Native American tribes, Voodoo practitioners, and certain segments of Buddhism, the dead and the living can coexist, and the dead can influence the well-being of the living. In some cases, people are forbidden from mentioning the names of the deceased in the fear it will prevent the ghost from leaving this earth and attaining peace. According to some Islamic teachings, the great Prophet Mohamed stated that the sins of a martyr will be forgiven when he sheds his first drop of blood. In addition, he can admit seventy relatives to paradise and will personally be married to seventy-two beautiful virgins upon his arrival there. Although this approach to death is said to be associated with the Islamic faith, this represents a clear case of how religion interacts with other aspects of culture and the rest of the world. The ripple effect of cultural and religious differences can be felt most severely in our present day. This is greatly felt by other people who are in fear of travel to the Middle East where the practice of suicide bombings seems to be localized despite the fact millions of practicing Muslims elsewhere do not proscribe to that thinking.

All cultures have an idea of how death should occur. Sadly, in most places in the United States it occurs in a sterile and cold environment, such as in nursing homes for the elderly, like my own grandmother, or in hospitals in which most people die quietly and often alone.

In these cases, the elders sometimes rarely know who is with them at the time of death being mentally out of it due to senility or medication. On the other hand, a good death to most people here in America is typically imagined to give time for personal closure with friends and family, and when the dying person attempts to complete unfinished tasks. This occurs when people are given the chance, such as when they are diagnosed with a terminal illness with a certain expected time period left until death. It is important to examine cultural variations in conceptions of death and dying because they have significant implications on how people act in life, how they approach death, whether or not they fear death, and on their funeral and bereavement practices.

Death Anxiety: The Fear of Death

Most people do not willingly welcome the idea of their own or their loved ones' deaths. Our most common reaction to the thought of dying is denial or fear—out of leaving loved ones, a loss of what is familiar, and fear of the unknown. No matter how solid one's belief is in a religion that assures them of reuniting with loved ones on the other side, fear, nevertheless, invades nearly everyone's minds. It is this fear of death that is a major motivator of behavior. When it is channeled properly, it becomes a motivating force to propel people to great achievements with the goal that those achievements would outlast their own life, through works of art, writing, acting careers, and so forth. This can be a positive force as people who are so driven are more likely to want to have children as their legacy, become a care provider or enrich the lives of others through great acts of kindness over a lifetime. However, the same death anxiety, if not well handled, can become a destructive force resulting in both physical and mental problems. The fear of death, of either themselves or of others, for some, can come from a fear of judgment—whether one would go to heaven or hell, the fear of burial, and what might happen to people and possessions that one may leave behind.

Fear of dying, in a personal regard, more often comes down to the fear of the *how*, because some people are not directly afraid of death itself. Some of our anxieties may be the loss of physical appearance and uses of bodily functions, and even the possible pain that may accompany dying. It is very common for the ill or elderly to worry about being a burden to others, both in terms of stress and financial costs. These fears are likely to manifest in various ways. Death anxiety is sometimes expressed through avoidance as people consciously refuse to attend funerals or visit friends and loved ones who are dying because it makes them feel uncomfortable. Some people avoid hospitals period. I myself feel closed in on by the cold sterile feeling of such places. From the pure white and bright light to the cold metal of institutions to the demeanor of staff, it is no wonder most people prefer to die in a familiar and safe place, such as at home surrounded by loved ones. Other people with certain types of personalities may display this death anxiety by engaging in activities that seem to either confront or directly defy death by repeatedly engaging in risky activities or career choices, like police or military. Others may cope with it more directly by getting jobs that deal with death by becoming involved with city morgues, funeral parlors, or retirement homes.

This anxiety is not the same in other cultures. Especially among religious people where the idea of an afterlife is reinforced, levels of death anxiety are decreased due to comfort found in salvation, or reuniting with those passed before them. Many of those in jails and prisons find religion while incarcerated. While I was doing artwork for the CD *Scribings of a Forgotten Soul* for the band URN, I was made more aware of this subject based on the story of the album. It is about a man on Death Row who finds solace in religion.

People of all belief systems have death anxiety—especially those who may question life after death. Most of the societies in the West are secular and in denial of our own mortality. People vow not to go without fighting illness, as we try to deny doctors prognosis when they tell us how much time we have left, we seek alternative medical practices from other cultures in hopes to stall the reaper.

Personally, I believe in the idea one must live life to its fullest. If a person of this mindset were to die, they will have had fewer regrets. Just watch Queen Latifah in the movie *Last Holiday*, and you'll see how one can forget about the daily grind and let go, by achieving true happiness and truly tasting the richness life has to offer.

GRIEF AND BEREAVEMENT

Events leading to death, such as terminal illness, do not always end with the death of the dying person. In fact, all humans, including the dying, experience grief as a response to impending death. Bereavement refers to the experiences that follow the death of a loved one, while mourning is the process through which grief is expressed. How people behave after a death differs from culture to culture. Some cultures expect close relatives to shave their heads, and, depending on the culture, wear either white or black clothing, and to express grief for a specified minimum period of time.

Universally accepted grief reactions that are commonly expressed are crying, fear, and anger. Grief and mourning involve a specific sequence, a process that consists of phases which include shock (disbelief and numbness), denial, bargaining, guilt, anger, depression, and acceptance. The feelings of shock are to protect the person from the severe pain of bereavement. The last phase, acceptance, is when people come to terms with the fact that the deceased is gone and never will return. Children may have a difficult or impossible time dealing with or accepting the loss of a parent or close friend, though some may grasp the concept of death, they may not completely understand it. Adults however cope with it in their own time, as they adjust to the loss of the deceased, and depending on the circumstances, try to find a reason why the deceased died. At last people are left with a severe sense of loss, and spend much time thinking about or dreaming about the deceased. When these feelings begin to fade, they move into the final stage of recovery, where they come to realize they need to move on in order to take care of themselves or children, jobs, and various other reasons, and slowly reenter society. The amount of time it takes different people to move from one part of the mourning process to the next greatly depends on a number of factors, such as the age at which the deceased died, the closeness of the relationship between them, and the availability of support the survivor has around them.

Chapter Two

Burial Rites of the World

"When you are born, you cry, and the world rejoices. When you die, you rejoice, and the world cries."

~ Tibetan Buddhist saying

While death is a topic largely avoided in Western culture, the remembrance of one's deceased ancestors and loved ones is traditional among diverse cultures around the globe, often marked by the lighting of candles or lamps and laying out offerings of food and drink. Such celebrations can be traced back as far as the glory days of ancient Egypt when departed souls were honored during the great festival of Osiris.

Death is universal and there are many common traits among death rituals spanning the globe. When examining death rituals cross-culturally, it is easy to attribute the same symbolic significance to similar rituals. Nevertheless, after looking at the rituals, used in the context of the culture they were created in, the symbolic meaning can be quite different.

Funeral and Burial Rituals

As with everything in the cycle of life, transitions occur and so, with people, rituals tend to accompany the many passages people go through. Some of these rituals include birthdays, graduations, and weddings. Death itself is the final transition and funerals are a rite of passage for both the dead and the living. Funeral rites or rituals act as a ceremony of honor for the deceased and assist the mourners to mentally process the passage of the dead. When people die, family and friends come together in order to deal with and mentally justify the cause of death and form a bond as survivors while, at the same time, in most cultures and faiths, attend a ritual designed to assist the dead in crossing over from one world into the next.

The Entombment, by artist Andreani, Andrea, ca. 1560-1623. The image shows Jesus Christ being supported by Joseph of Arimethia as Mary Magdalene gives comfort to the grieving Virgin Mary.

Funerals are much more than a symbolic closure to the end of someone's life. They help the living to grieve and go on with life. Families use each other as a support group, expressing their grief in a healthy manner as they readjust to life without a loved one. Each passing is different depending on the age of the deceased as well as how the death occurred and many other factors. When the death is of someone who has lived for a long time, a more festive feel is expressed, especially if it was a happy, fulfilled life. It tends to be more a celebration of that person's life, remembering all of the good times and how that person has touched their lives. However, the rituals that accompany the death of a child tend to be more somber.

In almost all countries it is universally accepted to release feelings by crying, or even expected on certain occasions, including funerals, to symbolize the attachment between the living and dead. The ritual of death addresses the absence felt for the loss of the person, and symbolic death rituals often are part of rites of passage marking other kinds of transitions. In secret societies such as the Masonic order, the initiate would "die" and be reborn as a member, so profound is the idea of death and transformation it is part of life. This idea of transformation is further pronounced by the initiate removing their clothing and then donning the robes of the order after their "rebirth." In these cases, death and rebirth are symbols for leaving one state of mind and being reborn into another.

Actual death is unique among rites of passage in the fact that we can never know the final state the dead enter at the end of the ritual, despite beliefs concerning the ultimate fate of the dead. Some people believe that a spirit will remain partly linked to the body, unless assisted to cross over. Most rituals include preparation of the dying person for passing. For Catholics, a priest will offer the terminally ill what is known as *Viaticum,* food for a journey; along with the Prayer of Commendation, which contains the phrase, "May the Lord Jesus Christ protect you and lead you into eternal life." This idea of food and possessions accompanying the dying into the afterlife is as old as mankind. It is a way to hold fast to the concept that there is an afterlife waiting for those left behind. Death rituals also serve as a way for people to have a chance to make amends, say goodbye and tell the deceased how much they love them.

As decades pass, the traditional funeral rite has evolved for many reasons, such as immigration of other cultures into the United States, the increased demand for cremations; and decline in religious practices with traditional rites giving way to more modern methods.

The typical funeral that is popular in modern day America is, however, a very recent ritual. In the past, funerals tended to be very plain, a pine box, family and friends caring for the body, and simple burial. This is in dramatic contrast to the modern funeral that is carried out by professionals who transform the dead body into a memorial.

Since the beginning of man, a wide variety of methods for interring the bodies of the dead have been used. First we'll examine the history of where remains were usually kept before moving on to the ceremonies of various traditions.

Opposite:
Catacombs in Rome,
Courtesy Library of Congress.

OSSUARY

An ossuary is a chest, building, or well that is used for the final resting place of human skeletal remains, used where burial space is scarce. First the body is buried in a temporary grave, then after some years the skeleton is removed and placed in an ossuary. In Persia, the Zoroastrians used a deep well for this same function nearly 3,000 years ago. This well was called "*astudan*" translating into "the place for the bones." Many examples of ossuaries are found within Europe such as the Santa Maria della Concezione dei Cappuccini in Rome, Italy, the San Bernardino alle Ossa in Milan, Italy, and the Sedlec Ossuary in the Czech Republic. The bones were then exhumed and stored in ossuaries, usually within the church, under the floor and behind the walls. The most famous ossuary, known for its incredible display of transposition of the remains around the building, is the Boney Church in Prague, where the skeletal remains of hundreds were turned into wall art and a chandelier. Another called the Capela dos Ossos, meaning "Chapel of Bones" can be found in the city of Évora, in Portugal. The village of Wamba, in the province of Valladolid, Spain, has an impressive ossuary of over a thousand skulls inside the local church, dating from between the twelfth and the eighteenth centuries. A more recent example is the Douaumont ossuary in France that contains the remains of more than 130,000 French and German soldiers that fell at the Battle of Verdun during World War I. One of the most famous is known as the Catacombs of Paris, from the eighteenth century, where thousands of human remains were transferred from graveyards all over the city. To this day, guided tours run visitors through to take pictures. The catacombs beneath the Monastery of San Francisco in Lima, Peru, also contain an ossuary.

Jewish burial customs included primary burials in burial caves, followed by secondary burials in ossuaries placed in smaller niches of the burial caves. Limestone ossuaries that have been discovered, containing intricate geometrical patterns and inscriptions identifying the deceased, date back over 1,000 years. Among the best-known Jewish ossuaries of this period is the ossuary inscribed "Simon the Temple builder" in the collection of the Israel Museum.

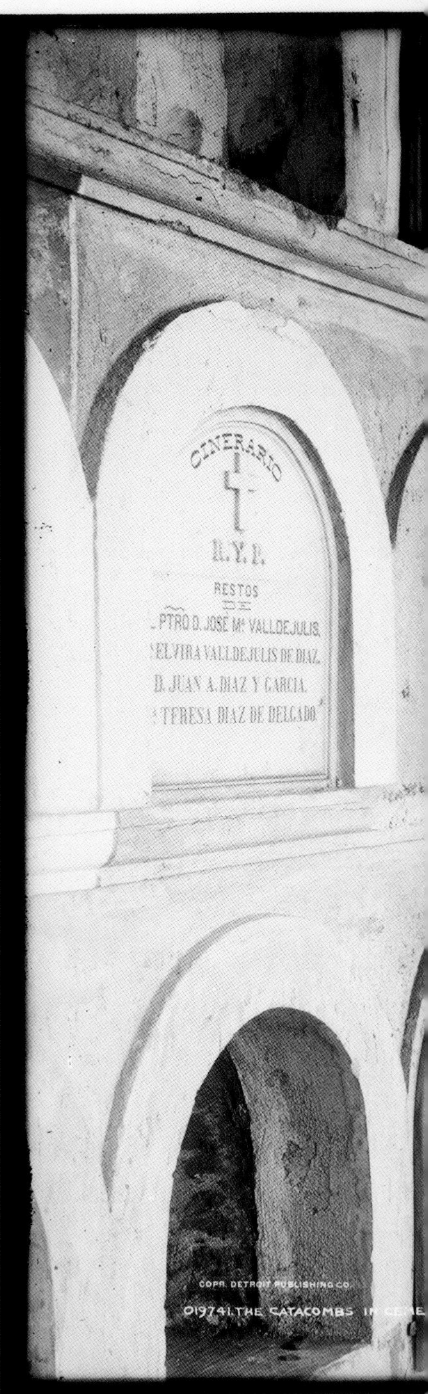

Charnel House

Much like an ossuary, a charnel house, used in the fourteenth century, was a vault or building where human skeletal remains were stored. These charnel houses, often built near churches, were built for depositing bones that were unearthed in order to store them while workers would commence digging a new grave. Also, this term can also be used more generally as a description of a place filled with death and destruction. Often occurring in particularly rocky places, where ground suitable for burial was scarce, corpses would be allotted a certain period of temporary interment following death. This enabled the relics to be harvested in houses that were made specifically for mortuary services. They offered privacy and shelter as well as enough workspace for mortuary proceedings, such as de-fleshing of the body before the cremation.

Catacombs in San Juan, *Courtesy Library of Congress.*

CRYPTS

The word crypt comes from the Latin *crypta* and Greek *kryptē*, which is a stone vault beneath the floor of a church usually used as a burial vault containing coffins. Originally, crypts were typically found below the main apse of a church, but were later located beneath the naves as well. Occasionally, churches were raised high to accommodate a crypt at the ground level, such as St. Michael's Church in Hildesheim, Germany. In some instances, remains were buried deeper, such as the case of Vlad Tepes (Dracula), and others in the area, whose remains are supposedly buried inside the main section of Snagov monastery.

Early Byzantium at Saint John Studio in Constantinople used crypts also. The most famous crypt is at Old St. Peter's Basilica, in Rome, built in the year 600, as a means of giving pilgrims a view of Saint Peter's tomb, which is directly below the high altar. The tomb was made accessible through an underground passageway beneath the sanctuary, where visitors could enter without disrupting parishioners. The usage of crypts increased in churches in the mid-eighth century, Western Europe under Charlemagne during the Romanization. Shortly after the tenth century, the early Medieval usage of a crypt faded, as church officials permitted ceremonies to be held in the main level of the church and the Gothic period crypts were rarely constructed anymore.

St. Bavon Abbey Crypt,
Courtesy Library of Congress.

Opposite:
Hythe church crypt,
Courtesy Library of Congress.

10911. HYTHE CHURCH. THE CRYPT.

Crypt in Provins France, *Courtesy Library of Congress*.

The Mausoleum at Halicarnassus

Since the Roman era, the term *mausoleum* has meant any large-scale tomb, though, it has very specific origins that can be traced back to one of the Seven Wonders of the Ancient World. The Mausoleum at Halicarnassus was an opulent tomb for a king who loved all things Greek. This tomb was the most monumental feat of art and architecture, in such size and scale, the world has ever seen before or since. It was built for *Maussollos*, the king of *Caria*, a province of the Persian Empire in the mid-fourth century B.C. Completed in 350 B.C., this tomb was thought to be built by Maussollos' wife and sister, Artemisia, in dedication of a grieving widow to her beloved husband. It now rests on the coast of Halicarnassus, the capital city.

This monument was designed by Greek architects Satyrus and Pythius, a testament to the Classical Greek architectural and artistic tradition. Maussollos and Artemisia worked to show off their capitol city of Halicarnassus by featuring a Greek theatre, temples to the gods, and planned for their entire city to be homage to Classical Greek art and architecture. They decorated buildings with magnificent columns of marble, and showcased Greek sculptural styles.

After Maussollos' death in 353 B.C., a devastated Artemisia commissioned famous Greek sculptors such as Bryaxis and Timotheus to create fantastic reliefs, enlisted Greek architect and sculptor Scopas to oversee construction, and hired hundreds of workers to finish the massive structure that measured 130 feet high, was surrounded by a wall, and had statues of the Greek gods around the courtyard. Stone warriors guarded the building at the four corners, and the marble tomb was centered on a platform and covered in detailed sculptures that depicted historical and mythical Greek battles. On top the roof was a pyramid upon which four horses pulling the former ruler, Maussollos, and Artemisia in a chariot. In 1494, the *Knights of St. John* used what remained of the mausoleum in order to fortify their castle at Bodrum. Next to nothing remained of the original, however, reconstruction of this unsurpassed achievement of artistic memorial to another living being was completed based on accounts of ancient writers, surviving sculptures and excavations of the area where the Mausoleum sat.

Burial Vaults

Like crypts, burial vaults became a trend in the 1800s. Burial vaults were usually crypts on medium to large size family estates that were subtly placed on the edge of the grounds or found beneath privately owned chapels, known as "family crypts." Family crypts were the place in which all members of the family became interred, often over centuries. When a crypt or burial vault was above ground, it was more commonly called a mausoleum. This term can also refer to any elaborate building used in place of burial. Around the seventh century, European burial was under the control of the Church and took place on holy ground. In Europe, bodies were usually buried in a mass grave until they had decomposed. Certain people who were vastly wealthy and of a high social stature, or extremely important professions, were usually buried in individual crypts inside or beneath the church with an inscription of the deceased, their date of death, and sometimes a short writing about them, complete with the family coat of arms.

Graveyards Replaced by Cemeteries

Graveyards were usually owned by the place of worship next to which they were created. The use of graveyards for burial of the dead was largely discontinued in towns until the nineteenth century when they were replaced by cemeteries. Among the reasons for this was a very sharp rise in the size of the population during the early stages of the Industrial Revolution. As populations grew and took over more land, there became a lack of space in graveyards for new burials of all those who were dying from infectious diseases. In large metropolises, like London and Paris, the concept was revolutionized with the design of elaborate garden cemeteries that were lushly landscaped burial grounds as well as public parks. As a consequence, governments, as well as places of worship, began to change burial regulations in both Europe and America alike. Sometimes, especially in southern states or old sections of Pennsylvania or New England, you can travel on the outskirts of cities and see old headstones in very small rustic graveyards. Few could afford the work of a stonemason who would be hired to create a headstone carved and set up over the place of burial, and only the wealthy continued to produce elaborate displays of death monuments for public show. Very similar to showing off their mansions and vehicles, many families used to compete for the artistic value of their headstone or vaults in comparison to others, which is why you see some families with huge angels amidst other smaller markers. Typically the lower class in those days, who could not pay for a headstone, had a simple wooden cross. However, these wooden crosses would quickly deteriorate because of harsh weathering over the years.

Arlington cemetery, *Courtesy of Library of Congress.*

Laurel Hill cemetery, *Courtesy of Dark Gothic Resurrected Magazine, 2010.*

Cemeteries

A cemetery is a place where dead bodies and cremated remains are buried. Unlike in graveyards in small towns, these new places of burial were established away from heavily populated areas and outside cities. This term originally was applied to the Roman underground cemeteries known as catacombs. The term cemetery, from the Greek κοιμητήριον, meaning sleeping place, implies that the land is specifically designated as a burying ground. Most Greek cities placed their cemeteries along the main roads outside the city walls in order to avoid disease and religious pollution, and perhaps even to avoid wasting valuable urban space. As the *Oxford English Dictionary* states, a cemetery is: *A burial-ground generally; now esp. a large public park or ground laid out expressly for the interment of the dead, and not being the "yard" of any church.*

Cemeteries, in the Western world, are the place where the final ceremonies for the dead take place.

Modern cemeteries, which are the most common places in America to place our loved ones after death, are now landscaped and have became owned by private companies or even non-profit cemetery organizations that are increasingly operating independently from churches, removed from any particular faith.

Caskets and Coffins

Caskets have been used in one form or another for almost as long as mankind has existed. The traditional coffin is much more than a simple container for the deceased to lie in. It was a demonstration of the value people placed on the dignity of the deceased on their final journey to the grave in a symbolic show of ritual.

Back in about 695, the Celts created caskets out of simple flat stones roughly in the shape of a box. Nobility across the world were buried in luxurious jeweled caskets, and during Victorian times, the wealthy in America were buried in solid-oak coffins with heavy brass fittings and elaborate ornamentations, while at the same time, the poor were carried to their graves in plain wooden coffins that would be reused over and over again. Caskets today are usually made of heavy steel. This began in 1885 when General Ulysses S. Grant was buried in a metal casket with a full plate glass top. Caskets still follow the traditional rectangle design and are still designed to be as airtight as possible.

Old west cemetery,
Courtesy Library of Congress.

Laurel Hill cemetery, *Courtesy of Dark Gothic Resurrected Magazine, 2010.*

May Be Creepy ... But True

Since their beginning, one of the reasons caskets existed was to preserve a body for as long as possible. Scientists have recently discovered, however, that bodies in airtight caskets tend to decompose more quickly than those in more open caskets.

Laurel Hill cemetery, *Courtesy of Dark Gothic Resurrected Magazine, 2010.*

Laurel Hill cemetery, *Courtesy of Dark Gothic Resurrected Magazine, 2010.*

Laurel Hill cemetery, *Courtesy of Dark Gothic Resurrected Magazine*, 2010.

As times and attitudes change, we now see a rise in popularity of cremation, with as much as seventy percent of funeral caskets made of combustible wood. Cremation, and lower-cost urns, are rapidly gaining market share, according to Robert Fells, spokesman for the International Cemetery, Cremation and Funeral Association.

Although some people cling to tradition and believe nothing but the best is still often felt to be the least a grieving relative can provide, the most basic chipboard, or even cardboard coffin is also now widely acceptable and most crematoriums allow them in order to be both inexpensive and for those who believe in environmental protection. Ironically, when we look at environmental issues, cardboard does use up more fossil fuels than slow-burning wood, and formaldehyde, used in the manufacture of chipboard, is hazardous when it burns. The coffin most commonly offered is chipboard veneered in oak or mahogany with handles that appear to be brass but are in fact made of a type of easily combustible material. Sometimes the funeral director will supply a rich velvet pall cover to cover the coffin during the service. Truth be told, the most environmentally friendly and economical "green" choice is untreated pine.

Laurel Hill cemetery, *Courtesy of Dark Gothic Resurrected Magazine, 2010.*

Caskets, especially the American style of coffin, are rectangular rather than the Halloween looking European taper-styled ones, typically with a split lid designed for viewing. They can be made of wood, steel, solid bronze or finished in white enamel covered oak.

Walmart has taken over almost every item people can conceivably need in life, and now even after that life is done, by putting caskets and other funeral supplies for sale on Walmart.com. This includes pet urns and memorial jewelry. Other none traditional retailers have also been selling caskets online for years, such as Costco and Amazon.

Books, too, are not to be outdone in the casket line. Robin Moore put together a compelling collection of Living Dead Doll memorabilia housed in a book shaped like a coffin called *Unauthorized Guide to Collecting Living Dead Dolls*. Caskets and other collectible items can be found, too, in the book *Postmortem Collectibles* by C. L. Miller.

While caskets are, of course, typically used for burial of the dead, some more eccentric people have used them for daily sleeping and other activities. Actress Sarah Bernhardt is rumored to take her "bed," a casket, with her when she travels, and famous psychic Criswell is said to sleep in caskets. The vampire, Don Henrie, shocked viewers on the reality show *Mad, Mad House* in 2004 doing the same, as have a few others such as on the television show, *Real Sex,* from HBO, that interviewed a vampire stripper. The rock band KISS had a coffin made, a high quality black one with the band's faces and logo on it as a novelty.

Unusual Coffins

As environmental concerns and individuality are becoming more visible at funeral services, some people are choosing to make their own coffins. "Funeral directors are increasingly likely to accept a homemade coffin from you as long as it meets the anti-pollution requirements," says the Natural Death Centre. Colorful Coffins offer families an additional choice when it comes to choosing a coffin for their loved ones. The company pioneered the customized picture coffins. This can involve the addition of family photographs, holiday pictures or even favorite hobbies or sports can be integrated into the design. This is a way for people to celebrate the life of the person they have lost, and people can even pre-design their own coffins if they so wish. Another company, Greenfield Creations offers a vast range of colors from plain white, black, wood grain to the highly popular marble effect finishes, although, by using digital print technology, they also specialize in offering personalized designs; all the family needs to do is provide a personal photograph or idea and they do the rest.

May Be Creepy ... But True

Body Shop founder Anita Roddick was buried in a recycled paper coffin called the Ecopod, which are biodegradable coffins shaped like a seed pod. They come in a variety of colors such as silver and gold leaf.

An increasingly popular choice is wicker or willow coffins. Being very eco-friendly as they are both carbon neutral and easily sustainable. Offered in a wide range of styles and colors, these innovative coffins can be purchased through buying direct from the manufacturers and having it delivered to the funeral director. The Natural Legacy Range by JC Atkinson, in partnership with Hainsworth Coffins, offers a unique design combining the highest of environmental standards. The Wharfedale is made using heavy organic cotton supported by a strong recycled cardboard frame and edged in jute, while the Swaledale is similar but uses soft wool, both of which are biodegradable. Coffin Cover is a high quality wooden shell that covers the actual simple, biodegradable coffin for the duration of the service. They use the same pauper ideal left over from Victorian times, and the cover is used repeatedly.

Laurel Hill cemetery, *Courtesy of Dark Gothic Resurrected Magazine, 2010.*

Laurel Hill cemetery, *Courtesy of Dark Gothic Resurrected Magazine, 2010.*

Laurel Hill cemetery, *Courtesy of Dark Gothic Resurrected Magazine, 2010.*

Laurel Hill cemetery, *Courtesy of Dark Gothic Resurrected Magazine, 2010.*

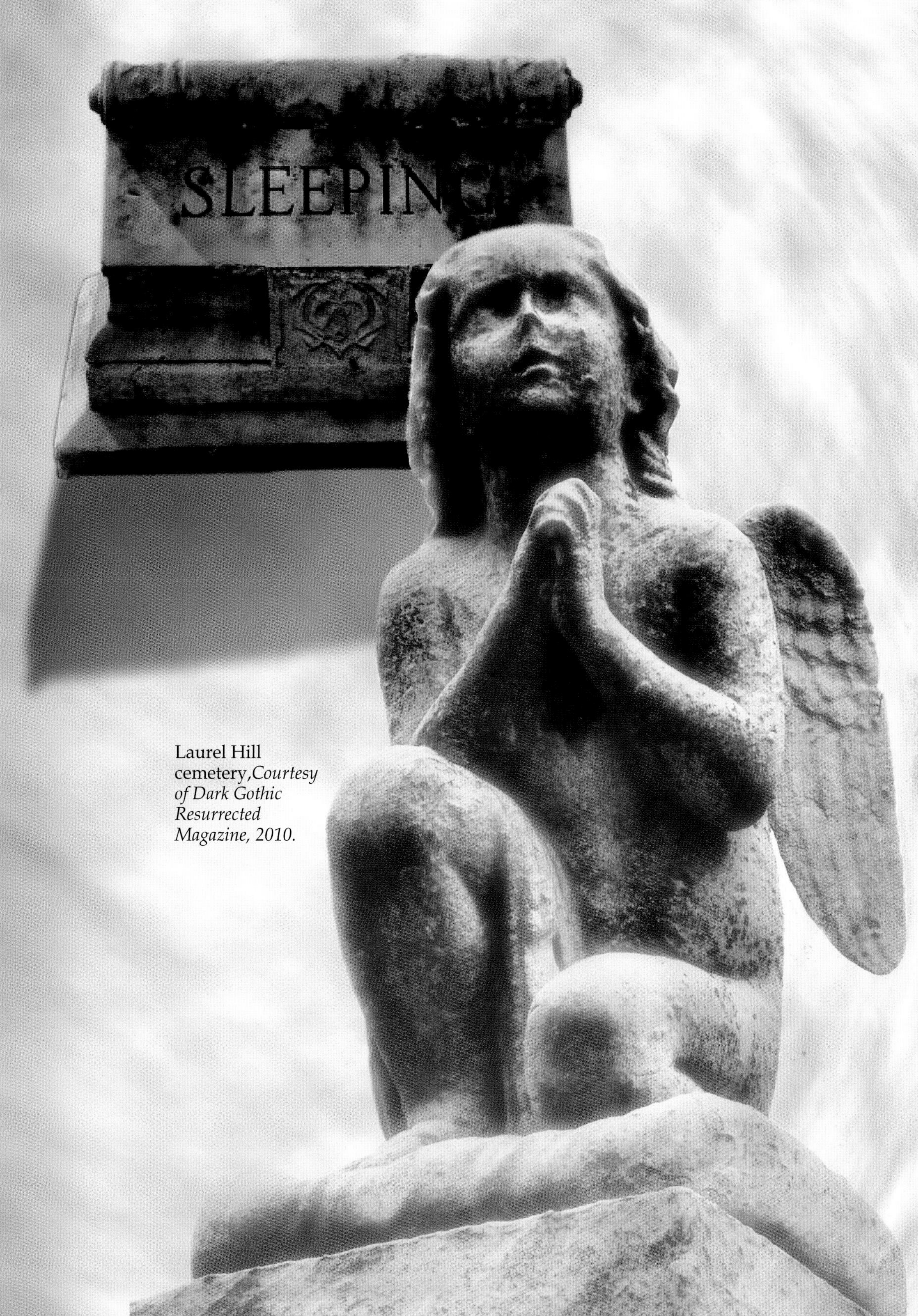

Laurel Hill cemetery,*Courtesy of Dark Gothic Resurrected Magazine, 2010.*

As the reflection in the photograph shows, we all must reflect back on our inevitable demise and hope the epitaph inscribed on this stone is one we are worthy of as well. *Author's commentary*

FISHER
FISHER
HOUSER

Local Fort Wayne cemetery in middle of two highways.

Tomb of the Unknown Soldier, *Courtesy Library of Congress.*

President James grave, Courtesy Library of Congress.

Urns and Keepsakes

Cremation-memorial urns are surprisingly not only used to keep ashes, it can hold a personal object, photograph, lock of hair, anything that is a personal reminder of the deceased. Many urn styles, shapes, and materials are used but most are in marble, bronze, or brass.

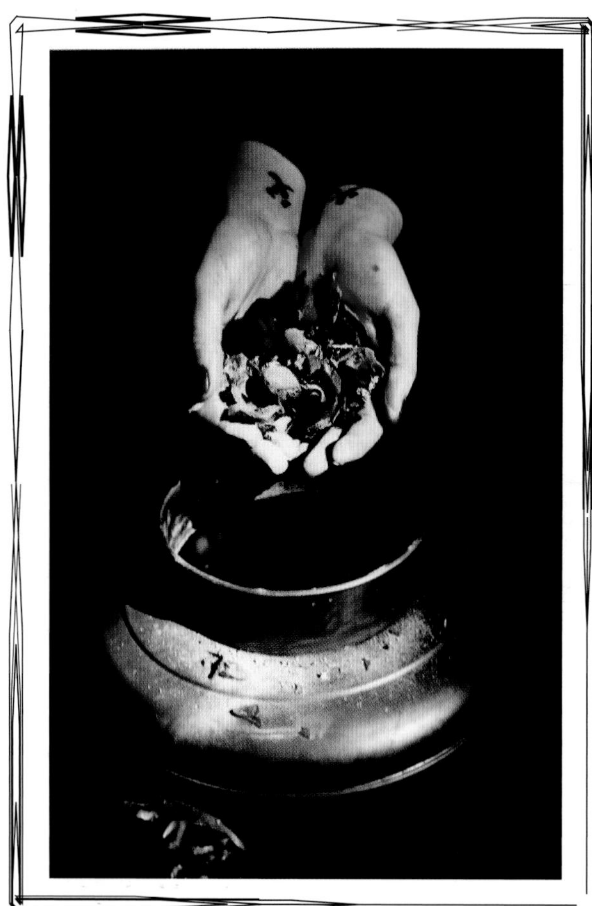

Urn, *Courtesy Pendragon Studios, 2008.*

Local Fort Wayne cemetery photo flower urns.

Egyptian Life After Death

The ancient Egyptians' attitude towards death was influenced by their belief in immortality. They regarded death as a temporary interruption, rather than the end of life. People paid homage to the gods, both during and after their life on earth, to ensure the continuity of life after death. The earliest ancient Egyptians buried their dead in small pits in the desert, where the combination of heat and dryness of the sand dehydrated the bodies quickly, and created lifelike and natural mummies. When they died, they were mummified so the soul would return to the body, giving it breath and life. Household equipment and food and drink were placed on offering tables outside the burial chamber to provide for the dead's needs in the afterworld.

Egyptians believed that there were six important aspects that made up a human being: the physical body, shadow, name, the ka (which means spirit), the ba (the personality), and the akh (which is immortality). Each one of these elements played an important role and was necessary to achieve rebirth into the afterlife. With the exception of the akh, all these elements join a person at birth. A person's shadow was always present, as the Egyptians believed a person could not exist without a shadow, nor the shadow without the person. The shadow was represented as a small human figure painted completely black (which is of more importance later when we get to the chapter on Goth).

People were named at birth and would live for as long as that name was spoken. The ka was a person's double, their spirit or soul, and was created at the same time as the physical body, by Khnum, the ram-headed god, on a potter's wheel. The ka existed in the physical world and resided in the tomb. It had the same needs that the person had in life, whereas the ba was, in effect, one's personality, entering a body with the first breath of life and it left at the time of death. It moved freely between the underworld and the physical world, and had the ability to take on different forms.

The akh was the aspect of a person that would join the gods in the underworld. It was immortal and unchangeable, created after death by the use of funerary text and spells, designed to bring forth an akh. Once this was achieved that individual was assured of not dying a second death, which would mean the end of someone's existence.

The ancient Egyptians believed that without a physical body there was no shadow, name, or any other element, so an intact body, however, had to be preserved as it was a highly critical part of a person's afterlife and needed for all eternity. The Egyptians believed that the human soul used the first night after death to travel into the afterlife.

Mummification

After burial in the desert pits became used less and less, the practice of burying the dead in coffins began in order to protect them from wild animals. However, they came to realize that bodies placed in coffins decayed when they were not exposed to the conditions of the hot, dry sand of the desert.

Over many centuries, the ancient Egyptians developed a method of preserving bodies, many of which have remained in near perfect condition today, so they would remain more lifelike. Egyptians believed they were assuring themselves a successful rebirth into the afterlife by the lengthy process known as mummification. This process took seventy-two days to perform during which time they completed the deceased's tomb. All of their worldly possessions and the *Book of The Dead* were carefully laid in the tomb. The body was taken to the tent known as "ibu," the "place of purification." There the embalmers wash the body with palm wine and rinse it with water from the Nile. After a cut in the left side of the body, these ancient morticians removed the internal organs. The liver, lungs, stomach, and intestines are washed and packed in natron as was the body. Natron is a natural substance that is found in abundance along the Nile River. It is made up of sodium carbonate, sodium bicarbonate (baking soda), sodium chloride (salt), and sodium sulfate (sulfuric acid). These act as a drying agent, drawing the water out of the body.

Next, the body was stuffed with dry materials such as sawdust, leaves, and linen. After forty days, the body is washed again with water from the Nile. Then, they covered it with oils to help the skin stay elastic. The dehydrated internal organs were then placed in hollow Canopic jars, made of wood or stone and buried with the mummy to symbolically protect the organs. Imsety, the human-headed god, looked after the liver. Hapy, the baboon-headed god, looked after the lungs. Duamutef, the jackal-headed god, looked after the stomach and Qebehsenuef, the falcon-headed god, looked after the intestines. The heart is not taken out of the body because they thought it was the center of intelligence and feeling and that the deceased would need it in the afterlife. A long hook was then used to mash the brain so that it could be pulled out through the nose.

Finally, the body is covered again with perfuming oils. First, the head and neck are wrapped with strips of fine linen, then the fingers and the toes are individually wrapped, the arms and legs are wrapped separately. In between the layers of wrapping, the embalmers place amulets to protect the body in its journey through the underworld. The priest reads aloud spells, to help ward off evil as the deceased makes the journey to the afterlife, while the mummy is being wrapped. Protection spells written in hieroglyphs on coffins, were thought to help protect the deceased person and keep them safe on their journey through the underworld.

Mummy, *Courtesy Library of Congress.*

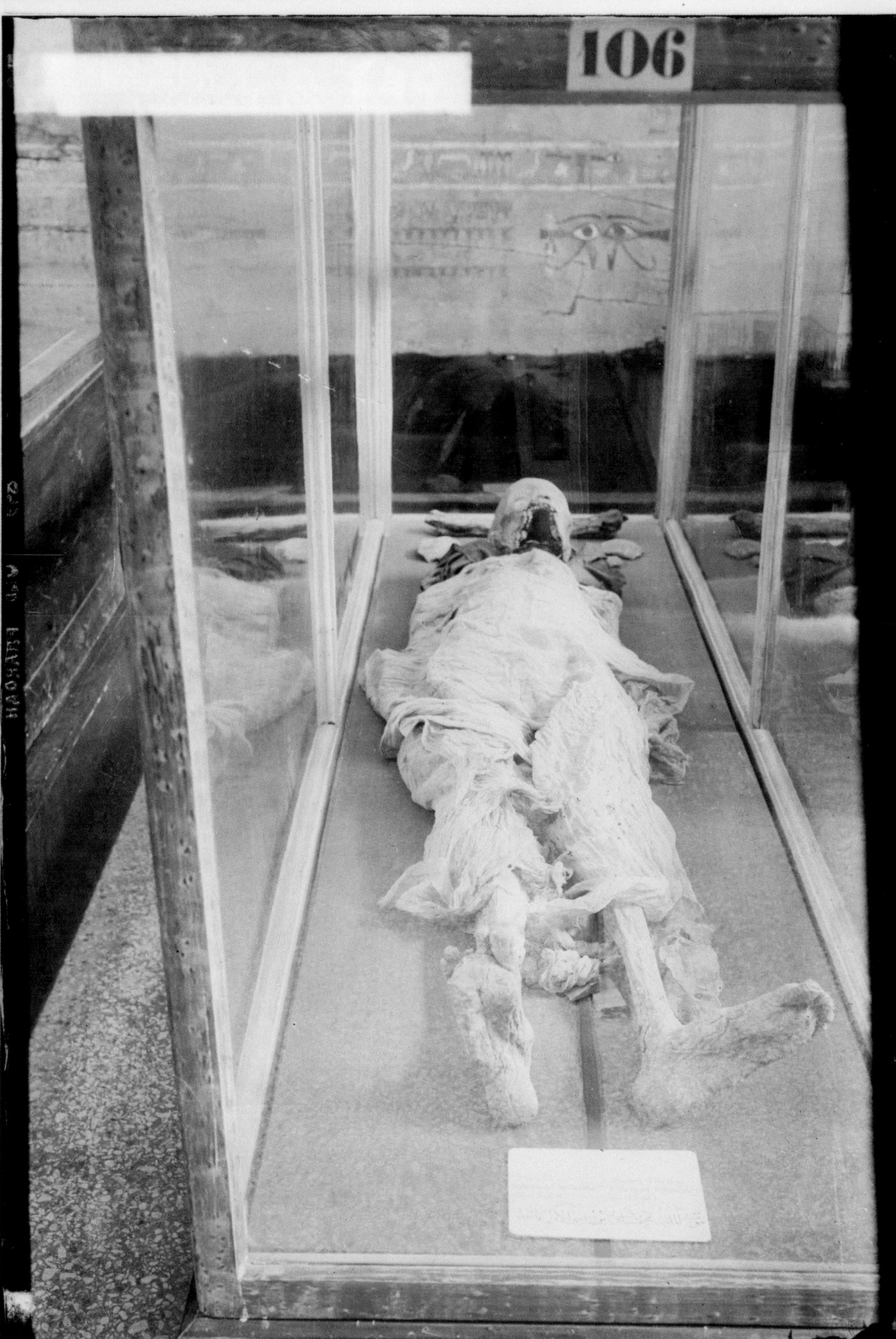
106

Tomb in Egypt, *Courtesy Library of Congress.*

Cairo Mummies, *Courtesy Library of Congress.*

Peru mummies, *Courtesy Library of Congress.*

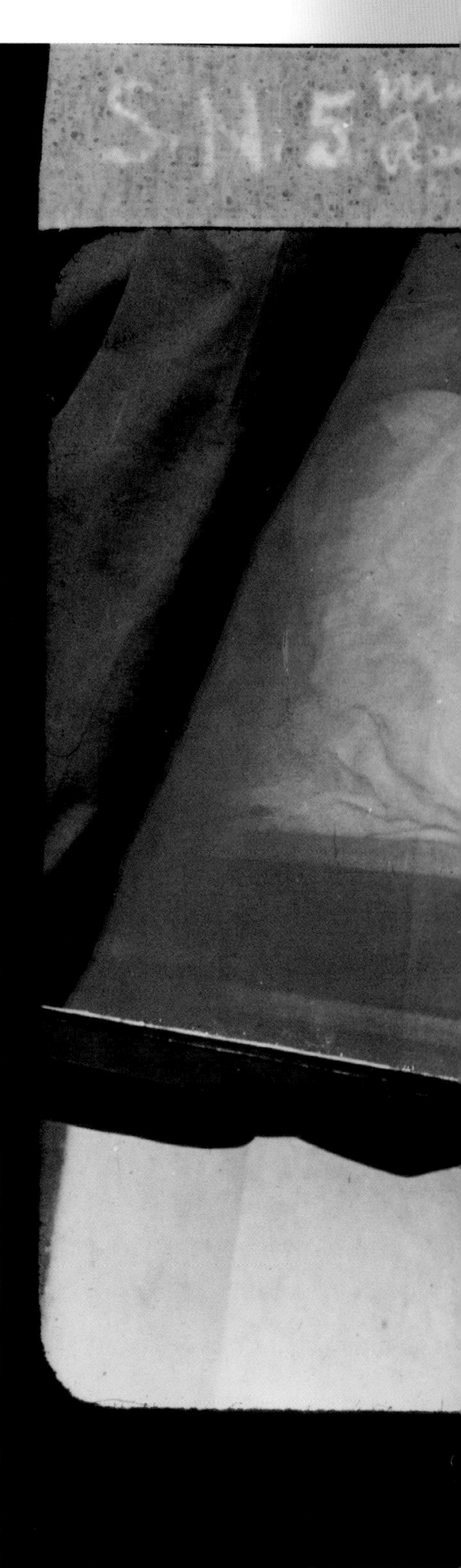

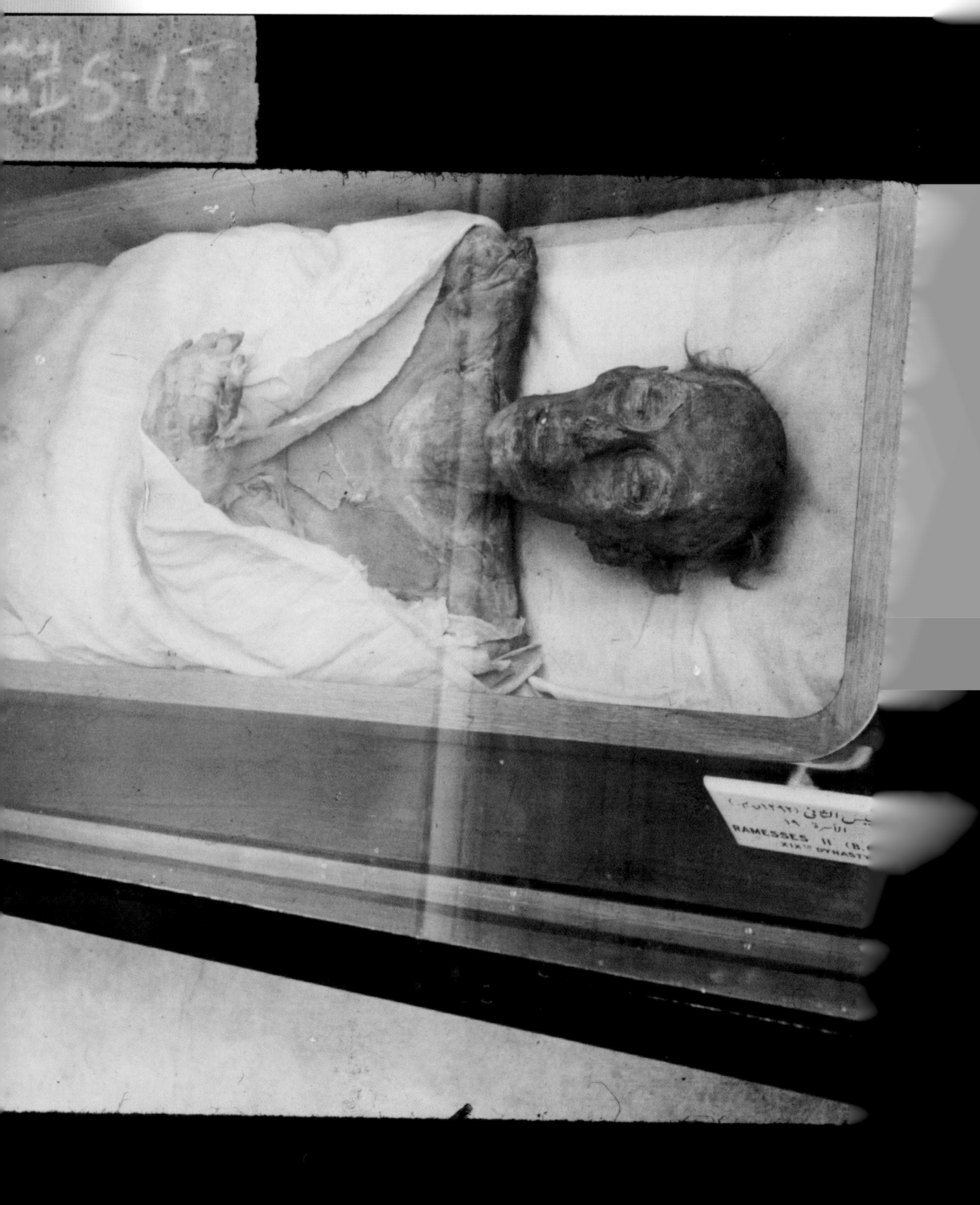

Pharaoh Ramses III, *Courtesy Library of Congress.*

H. C. WHITE CO., CHICAGO, NEW YORK, LONDON.
Gen'l Office and Works, North Bennington, Vt., U. S. A.
B

Mummies 30 to 40 centuries old, *Courtesy Library of Congress.*

The Book of The Dead

Although there are two cultures that have such a tome, the Egyptian and the Tibetan, I will explain each separately.

Egyptian

The Egyptian *Book of The Dead* is a set of spells, incantations, prayers, and preservation techniques designed to help the dead person resurrect into a glorious afterlife in "The Hall of the Two Truths" as it was known. It was illustrated and written on papyrus. *The Book of The Dead* can be thought of as the guidebook for the deceased to a happy afterlife as the text was intended to be read by the dead during their journey into the Underworld. Perhaps this is where Director Tim Burton got the idea for his *Handbook for the Recently Deceased* in his classic movie *Beetlejuice*, starring Michael Keaton. Indeed, both the Egyptian and Tibetan books showed how to overcome obstacles, revealed routes, gave clues to shortcuts, taught passwords and prayers to navigate safely, and kept the dead from otherwise losing their way—although, of course, the original also guaranteed the help and protection of the gods while proclaiming the deceased's identity with those gods.

These papyri books were commissioned by the wealthy well before their deaths and, depending on their prestige, the ruling class would naturally call for the finest quality papyrus that money could buy. The less affluent Egyptians would simply purchase a generic *Book of The Dead* and have a scribe fill in the blanks with their name.

Tibetan

Among the traditions of the Buddhist monks, Tibetans believe life has a cycle of death and rebirth, and one's consciousness remains afterward in an intermediate stage, called bardo, for forty-nine days. The deceased are attended by monks that chant and read from their *The Book of the Dead*, similar to the ancient Egyptians. After lighting lamps, they present offerings of food and drink. By using astrology, the proper manner and timing of disposal is determined.

In the shrine, found in every Tibetan household, can be found the pictures and objects necessary for the bardo ritual. For the death ritual, a small picture of the Buddha is included. Buddha is the most important figure in their deities, being the primordial image of all emanations from the sphere of the pure "dharmakaya." Other sacred figures or deities of Buddhism are also displayed, along with scroll paintings that are hung up, depicting peaceful and wrathful deities.

Ceremonies for monks who have died are even more elaborate, and, for the death rituals, the Mahakala dances are performed by monks in black robes accompanied by music. The bodies were venerated and preserved. To dispel fears about death, the monks used skeletons in art and skull drums, bowls and thigh bone instruments in the ritual. The altar is decorated with flowers. Bowls of water, sacrificial cakes, incense, and fruit are arranged in front of the ritual pictures. Sometimes, in addition to the usual candles, sacrificial lamps are used, made of brass, copper, or silver, in rows in front of the sacrificial bowls. Included among the items on the altar might be the offerings of the five senses and eight sacrificial gifts that bring good. Even a rice mandala may be used as the symbolic offering of all precious gifts of this impermanent world to the Buddhas.

First, at least two or more monks arrange the ritual objects on the narrow tables in front of which they sit. In the tantric ritual for the bardo deities, these are the ritual bell, the small hand-drum made of wood or skull-bone with hide stretched on both sides, the pair of small cymbals, a bowl of yellow sacrificial rice, and the ritual jug for consecrated water. This ritual jug is a vessel of sacred water and is of symbolic significance for the introduction into the teachings concerning the visions of the deities of the Tibetan *Book of the Dead*. In the upper opening of the vessel rests a crown of peacock feathers on a stick, used as a sprinkler. A final indispensable part of the ritual are the small cards with pictures of the deities of the *Book of the Dead,* which the monk holds in his hand. With these cards, they guide the deceased and portray, in separate groups, all the deities in an order corresponding to the *Book of the Dead*. These cards are shown and explained one at a time during the ritual, as the presiding lama holds them up at certain points in the text, and are the initiations for the dead.

However, without the presence of the dead person, the recitation of the *Book of the Dead* cannot begin. The most interesting and dramatic part of the whole death ritual is the initiation and conversation with the deceased through his image, the Byang-bu. In several verses, the deceased is called upon by the lama and entreated to appear from the bardo beyond and to take their place in the picture that has been prepared for them, so that they can take part in the ceremony. The deceased becomes present again, now symbolically beginning the journey through the six worlds. At the end, the picture is burned, symbolizing a second death on a higher, ritual, plane whereby the earthly death of physical decay is overcome.

Tibetan Sky Burial

Sky burial has been around since at least the twelfth century. This custom has remained in practice, but quite often the remains were cremated as monks, nuns, and mourners chanted mantras or prayers while being taken to the internment area. The bodies are laid out for carrion birds, and bones would be pounded into meal for them (see raven, crows, and vultures in the next chapter) as corpses were sliced up. Monks then set about the body with axes, laughing and joking as they do so. Then, wrapped in white cloth, the remains are bought to the burial site, where the monks leave them to airborne scavengers, usually in high, rocky places. This underlines the fact that Tibetans consider the body merely a vessel to be placed, usually, atop a mountain and left for the birds. Tibetans call the practice jhator, which means "giving alms to the birds."

Self Mummification

I found the ritual of self mummification one of the most disturbing of all. It was a form of slow suicide, practiced until the late 1800s in Japan, in accordance with the Buddhist idea that to achieve enlightenment one must separate the self from the physical world entirely so that at death, instead of being reborn, you become one with Buddha. This ritual took over 2,000 days of preparation, starting with the fat in the body being eliminated by changing the diet. The priests would eat only a small amount of nuts, bark, and roots from pine trees. They sought to remove as much moisture from their body as possible. Since the body is mostly moisture, this caused extreme discomfort. Near completion of their tomb, the monk would drink a poisonous tea made from the sap of an urushi tree, causing explosive diarrhea and vomiting, which was a step in further reducing the amount of moisture in the body. The sap-soaked the internal organs which lined them, protecting them against maggots. Finally they were sealed in a small, stone room just large enough to sit in the lotus position.

HINDU

Self-immolation, or Suttee, was a traditional Hindu ritual practiced in India, whereby a grieving widow will voluntarily lie next to her husband's side on his funeral pyre. She was, of course, burned alive next to the corpse. Widows were considered impure and something to be shunned. It was also believed that the husband and wife could be reunited after death, which is why sometimes the husband's most cherished possessions were burnt so that he could have them in the afterlife. Suttee had been practiced throughout India for centuries, before it was outlawed by the occupying British in 1829, even though some occurrences have persisted until the present day, causing it to be banned again in 1956, and again in 1981. Often, however, the woman would try to run away. This was considered highly dishonorable, so bystanders would jab the widow with bamboo canes or tie her down to keep her on the fire.

MAY BE CREEPY ... BUT TRUE

In an eighteenth-century incident of Suttee, when one widow got beyond the pokers and doused the flames in a nearby river, the onlookers threw her back onto the pyre after breaking her legs and arms.

Ancient Roman and Greek

The ancient Greek conception of the afterlife and the ceremonies associated with burial were already well established by the sixth century B.C. The Greeks believed in an afterlife as detailed in the classical tale *Odyssey*, by the writer Homer. He describes the Underworld, deep beneath the earth, where Hades reigned over the milling hordes of shadowy figures, called shades, the spirits of all those who had died.

The Greeks felt that at the moment of death the psyche left the body as a little breath or puff of wind to enter the realm of Hades. It had fled the body and now existed merely as a phantom image, perceptible but untouchable. Ancient literary sources emphasize the necessity of a proper burial and refer to the omission of burial rites as an insult to human dignity. Relatives of the deceased, primarily women, conducted the elaborate burial rituals. After being washed and anointed with oil, the body was dressed and placed on a high bed within the house. Then other relatives and friends came to mourn and pay their respects. This was featured in early Greek art when vases were decorated with scenes portraying the deceased surrounded by mourners. Following the viewing, the deceased was brought to the cemetery in a procession, which usually took place just before dawn. Monumental rectangular built tombs, sometimes very elaborate marble pieces decorated with statues, were often erected to mark the grave and to ensure that the deceased would not be forgotten.

Similar to headstones of today, the funerary monument had an inscribed base with an epitaph, a verse that memorialized the dead. Often a carved relief depicting a generalized image of the deceased sometimes decorated the burial site as well.

Jewish Funeral and Mourning Customs

From birth to death, the Jewish reflect on their existence and are grateful for life lived rather than mourn death. Judaism's response to death comes from its traditions beginning nearly 3,000 years ago. Its tenets emphasize a celebration of life and in providing comfort to the survivors. Indeed, psychologists believe this approach is most healthy and expedient in dealing with grief. It is customary for them to transport the deceased directly from the home to the cemetery. They do not file death certificates or get burial permits. Jewish tradition has developed a complete and pragmatic response to death.

May Be Creepy ... But True

Everything the Jewish do is designed to celebrate and appreciate life. Every prayer recited speaks of life and gratitude. The Kaddish, recited in memory of the dead, never mentions the word death. The Jewish funeral customs include Mitzvot of Bikur Cholim, the act of kindness of visiting the sick, and Kavod Ha-Met, honoring the dead, as Judaism equates a dead body with that of a damaged Torah scroll, no longer fit for its intended use, but still deserving reverence for the holy purpose it once served. This is why, from death to burial, the body is never left unattended and the soul is prayed for by a religious watchman, known as the Shomer.

In addition to the physical cleansing and preparation of the body for burial, a ritual called Chevra Kadisha is performed, a recitation of required prayers asking God for forgiveness for any sins that may have been committed by the person who died, for guarding over the person, and to grant them eternal peace. The prayers also express gratitude for the life of the deceased and all the good that has come as a result of this person's life. The Chevra Kadisha also performed the meaningful task of purifying the body, usually on the morning of burial, with a ritual bath called the Taharah. To quote the biblical verse in Ecclesiastes, "As he came, so shall he go." In other words, as a newborn child is immediately washed and enters the world clean and pure, they wanted a person who departs this world be cleansed and made pure.

Following the recitation of the prayers required for Taharah is a 2,000-year-old tradition of burial in shrouds called a Takhirkhin, preceding the placement of the deceased in the casket. Chevra Kadisha is a Holy Society who prepares the body for burial, and the Taharah performs the purification. Last is the service and prayers by the family and friends. The most well known, is Shiva. Shiva means seven in Hebrew and is a seven-day mourning period that begins after burial. Survivors concentrate on their inner feelings to begin the healing process and take the first step into re-entering normal life without the deceased.

My best friend and PR manager's mother died as I completed this book and he told me that the seven-day candle was burned as a symbol of eternal life and is placed in the eastern most part of the home facing toward Israel. Another Jewish custom is that dirt from Israel, their homeland, be tossed into the casket at the time of burial so that the deceased is still buried on Israeli soil. There are few or no open caskets because the Jewish people believe one should be buried as they came into the world and so there is no embalming of the body, no makeup, and only a shroud to clothe them. The seven-day candle is given, by the rabbi, to the closest kin of the deceased which is usually the family member that handles the eulogy and final arrangements.

The Catholic Church

Catholic priests prepare for funeral, *Courtesy Library of Congress.*

The Funeral Rites of the Roman Catholic Church recognize that the occasion of the family's viewing of the body of the deceased at a funeral home can be an emotionally difficult event, and so they conduct a brief prayer service to support mourners at the funeral home. The church does recognize the delicate situation of even suicide cases, although considered a sin, and, nevertheless do pray for the dead.

Death Rituals Among Muslims

In the Muslim faith, the dying is read a chapter from the Qu'ran and a few drops of holy water are given. After death, the body is then bathed several times, as in the Jewish, Egyptian, and Roman traditions, then anointed with perfume and draped in a seamless white shroud. The Muslim custom states that the body should be respected and not harmed in any way, and be buried within twenty-four hours of death. For followers of Islam, as with many other faiths, death is the end of life on this earth and the beginning of a life hereafter, stating, "Death is not final, but a temporary separation from the beloved person, who will be brought back to life on the Day of Judgment and, if God wills, be reunited with his family once more." They feel that burying a dead body and covering it is a collective obligation.

Mexico's Day of the Dead

November 1st, known as All Saints Day, and November 2nd called All Souls Day are marked throughout Mexico with colorful adornments, lively reunions at family burial plots, the preparation of special foods, offerings laid out for the departed on commemorative altars, and religious rites that include fireworks. They have no qualms about getting up close and personal with death, almost as if they deal with death by mocking it, considering it almost as if it were a person.

The first day of November is set aside for remembrance of deceased infants and children, and who are referred to as little angels. Those who have died as adults are honored the next day. From mid-October through the first week of November, shops all over Mexico are full of items for the Dia de los Muertos (Day of the Dead). These include all manner of funny skeletons and other macabre toys; elaborate wreaths and crosses decorated with paper or silk flowers; candles and votive lights; and fresh seasonal flowers, Among this is also edible offerings of skulls, coffins and the like made from sugar, chocolate, and sugary sweet rolls called pan de muerto (bread of the dead) that come in various sizes invariably topped with bits of dough shaped like bones. All of these goods are destined for the buyer's offering to the dead. If you watch the movies *The Crow; City of Angels,* or *Once Upon A Time in Mexico,* they show this at the end of both films.

At home, members of the family might decorate an altar elaborately in honor of deceased relatives, using candles, flowers, photographs of the departed, candy skulls inscribed with the name of the deceased, and a selection of his or her favorite foods and beverages. The offerings are then laid out in an artistic and fairly symmetrical fashion. The smell of burning copal (incense) and the light of numerous candles are intended to help the departed find their way. Often included are bottles of beer or tequila, cups of coffee, and fresh water, as well as platters of rice, beans, chicken, and breads. This sort of feast is also laid out again as spirits of the dead are expected to pay a holiday visit home as sustenance for the journey back and forth. The offering may also include cigarettes for former smokers, or toys and extra sweets for deceased children.

Relatives spruce up each gravesite at the family burial plot in the local cemetery, and they set about giving tombs a fresh coat of paint after making any necessary structural repairs, followed by being decorated according to local custom. The tomb may be adorned simply by a cross or elaborately embellished with colorful wreaths while graves of children are decorated with brightly colored festive adornments like paper streamers.

On November 2nd, family members gather at the cemetery for gravesite reunions bringing along picnic baskets and bottles of tequila for toasting the departed while mariachi bands lead heartfelt sing-alongs. Merchants set up stands outside the cemetery gates to sell food and drinks. Fireworks announce the commencement of an open-air memorial mass before the festivities begin. It is not unusual to find all-night candlelight vigils in cemeteries as relatives gather while the glow of thousands of votive candles illuminates the way for the departed. At midnight, they are called home with the mournful tolling of bells, as each soul is lovingly remembered with recitations of the Rosary.

The Ancient Aztec

Death has always held a significant place in the rituals of Mexico's ancient civilizations. Among the Aztecs, for example, it was considered a blessing to die in childbirth, battle, or human sacrifice, for these assured the victim a desirable destination in the afterlife. They believed death was an integral part of daily life and was considered just a further stage in the continuation of life towards the individual's final resting place. Among the Incans, the custom throughout Peru was to bury the bodies of the dead with all of their most prized possessions and with their most beautiful and best-loved women.

China

In Southern Chinese culture, graves are opened after a period of several years. The bones are removed, cleaned, dried, and placed in a ceramic pot for reburial. This practice is called digging up bones, and is an important ritual in the posthumous care taking of children for their deceased parents and ancestors. Failure to carry out this ritual is considered a failure of filial piety, one of the virtues, which is respect for the parents and ancestors, which means to be good and take care of one's parents; to engage in good conduct not just towards parents but also outside the home so as to bring a good name to one's ancestors; display courtesy; ensure male heirs, uphold fraternity among brothers; including display sorrow for their sickness and death; and carry out sacrifices after their death.

Ancient Barrows

Across the countryside of the British Isles are thousands of ancient grave mounds, known as barrows. They can be clustered together or miles apart, in deserted moors or standing beside a busy road. The custom of constructing barrows or mounds of stone or earth over the remains of the dead was a characteristic feature of the sepulchral systems of primitive times. Originating as a memorial to honor the memory of the dead, it continued through all the stages of culture that preceded the introduction of Christianity.

The primary idea of this type of burial was the provision of a housing for the dead; and so the barrow included a chamber or chambers where the deceased was surrounded with the prized possessions of his previous life. A common feature of the earlier barrows is the enclosing fence, which marked off the site from the surrounding ground. When the barrow was of earth, this was done by an encircling trench or if it was a stone structure, the enclosure was usually a circle of standing stones. Sometimes, instead of a chamber formed above ground, the barrow covered a pit excavated for the interment underground.

Usually, in England the long barrow contained a single chamber and mourners entered a passage underneath the higher and wider end of the mound. The long barrows of Great Britain are often from 200 to 400 feet in length by 60 to 80 feet wide, rough but strongly built. Belas Knap is a famous tomb dating back from around 1400 B.C. Thirty-eight skeletons were discovered in the tomb, and these and other artifacts can be seen in the folk museum in Winchcombe.

In Scandinavia, the construction of the chambers consists of five or six monoliths supporting one or more with the covering mound, or over which no covering mound has been raised. These were found in France as well. People would leave ornate vessels of clay for food and drink in the afterlife.

Before the long barrow, the custom of burning the body began back in the Stone Age. In the north of Scotland, Denmark, and in Ireland, around A.D. 1100, these barrows were royal cemeteries of the tribal confederacies with the round barrow or chambered cairn being from the earliest Pagan period till the introduction of Christianity. Later, the practice of cremation lead to the modification of the barrow structure. The chamber was no longer regarded as a habitation for the dead, but the holding place for the urn which held their ashes, especially around the Bronze Age. Beautiful implements and weapons, personal ornaments made of gold, amber, jet, and bronze were commonly buried with the dead.

Later, the custom changed, in Scandinavia, from barrows on land to that of burying Vikings onboard their ship, with a barrow on it, as discovered in Norway. One in particular was over seventy feet long with mast and sixteen pairs of oars. The body of the Viking, with his weapons, twelve horses and six dogs was also found.

Native Americans

Similar to the barrows found in ancient Great Britain were those of the Great Plains tribes of North America. The dead were buried in mounds of enormous magnitude. Often they were cremated with implements, weapons and ornaments of stone and bone, as well as pottery. The most famous of all are the chambered mounds situated in the eastern part of Clay County, on both sides of the Missouri River. The chambers are about eight feet square, nearly five feet high, and each chamber has passageways several feet in length. The walls of the passages were around several feet thick, made of stones without mortar. The top of one of the chambers was covered with large, flat rocks, but some were covered with wood. The inner chambers were filled with burnt clay and, under the burnt clay, in each chamber, were found the remains of several human skeletons, all of which had been burnt. It is quite possible, indeed probable, that these chambers were used for secondary burials, the bodies having first been cremated.

Indian Burying grounds, *Courtesy Library of Congress.*

MAY BE CREEPY ... BUT TRUE

Since the earliest periods of time, natural and artificial holes have been used as places of burial for the dead by American Indians. Nearly every state has uncovered burial caves with urn-burial.

THE LAST SCENE OF THE LAST ACT OF THE SIOUX WAR.—DRAWN BY H. F. FARNY.

Native scaffold, *Courtesy Library of Congress.*

SCAFFOLD BURIAL

Some Native Americans bury in the open air, instead of under the ground, for the purpose of protecting their dead from wild animals. Even more common than cave burial was the tree or scaffold burial, which was seven or eight feet high, and up to ten feet long. Built with forked ends on all four posts, and completed with flooring made of small poles. The body is then carefully wrapped in robes or blankets, dressed in the best clothing they owned, closely sewn up, and then fastened in the branches of a tree so high as to be beyond the reach of animals while their weapons, and personal belongings or small toys with them, if it was a child, and laid to rest on the poles. Like other cultures that leave food for the deceased, the tribe left buckets and baskets hanging from the posts. Finally, they sang what was known as the death-song, which was a recounting of the virtues and prowess of the dead. After which the oldest male addresses the Great Spirit, to welcome the deceased into the happy hunting grounds. Usually, the women relatives would locate a spot near where the body rested, and would keep up a wailing known as keening, often for a month.

IN SUMMARY

Even though all humans will eventually experience death, the conceptions about death and how we respond to it vary widely across cultures, as we have discovered. Despite the differences, there are as many similarities that all people seem to share, even if centuries passed before any evidence shows different cultures even met. As our world is increasingly shrinking due to the speed of technology and as people from cultures across the world connect by things as simple as an I-Phone or the Internet, and we have things like the Internet's Babel Fish to translate languages in seconds, it is nevertheless just as important, if not more so, to understand the age-old fears that surround the issues of death, just as we do the issues of life. This will better prepare us to understand people from other cultures as well as ourselves, so that their lives and ours may be enriched in the process.

Chapter Three

Death, Symbolism and the Psyche

"The boundaries between life and death are at best shadowy and vague. Who shall say where one ends and where the other begins?"
~ Edgar Allen Poe

All cultures have their own ways of dealing with their fears of death, and in some ways I think the fear slowly becomes more acceptable as humanity finds comfort by going so far as to personify this frightening idea into something identifiable, and in naming a concept as something like "The Grim Reaper," they can confront in their minds. Death itself then has been given a form, as certainly as did the ancient gods of all cultures. From the ancient philosophers in Greece, the concept of Thanatos, which is the personification of death and mortality in Greek mythology sprang up. The Greek poet Hesiod established in his Theogony that Thanatos is a son of Nyx (Night) and Erebos (Darkness) and had a twin named Hypnos (Sleep).

> And there the children of dark Night have their dwellings, Sleep and Death, awful gods. The glowing Sun never looks upon them with his beams, neither as he goes up into heaven, nor as he comes down from heaven. And the former of them roams peacefully over the earth and the sea's broad back and is kindly to men; but the other has a heart of iron, and his spirit within him is pitiless as bronze: whomsoever of men he has once seized he holds fast: and he is hateful even to the deathless gods.

Homer also confirmed Hypnos and Thanatos as twin brothers in his epic poem, *The Iliad*. Thanatos was a harbinger of suffering and grief, and his coming was marked by pain. But other Greek artists did not often follow this grim conception of Death.

In later eras, Thanatos came to be seen as a beautiful creature known as Ephebe, which became associated with a gentle passing, and not as a sorrowful end to life. Roman art depicted him as a winged boy, similar to Cupid. Around 438 BCE, he is dressed in black and carrying a sword, which then carried forward into the modern depictions of the cloaked and skeletal Grim Reaper version we are all so familiar with. This is where the word Thanatophobia came from, the fear of things associated with death, corpses, or graveyards.

Death's Breath, graphic art by Drake Mefestta, *Courtesy Ticia Martyr Image Photography, 2010.*

MAY BE CREEPY ... BUT TRUE

The academic and scientific study of death among human beings is known as Thanatology. It investigates the circumstances surrounding a death, the grief experienced by family and friends, as well as social attitudes towards death with ritual and memorialization frequently by professionals in nursing, psychology, sociology, psychiatry, or social work. This field describes changes that accompany death and the after-death period, such as stages of decomposition and decay. This is described in great detail by noted forensics author Katherine Ramsland who wrote *Cemetery Stories: Haunted Graveyards, Embalming Secrets and the Life of a Corpse After Death*. Thanatos often appears in popular culture, Death has become used as characters in various fictional works, and in anime and video games.

DANCE MACABRE

In Medieval Europe, artistic depictions of death called *Dance of Death*, also known as *La Danse Macabre*, depicted dancing cadavers which signified that no matter one's station in life, it is the dance of death that unites all people. This woodcut consists of the personified figure of death leading a row of dancing figures from all walks of life to the grave, an emperor, a youth, and a young woman, all as skeletons. This art reminds people of how fragile their lives were, using illustrated sermon texts from Paris in 1424. The most famous was a woodcut simply titled *Dance Macabre*, from 1493.

Terrors abounded in the minds of people during the fourteenth century, as great famines swept throughout Europe and the known world along with The Crusades and the Black Death. The omnipresent possibility of sudden and painful death increased the religious desire for salvation, as well as reminding people of the inevitability of death. Plays emerged in the wake of these events as a coping mechanism, and to prepare churchgoers for the inevitability of death. Usually, the performance took place in a cemetery or churchyard and dramatized a victim's meeting with death, personified as a skeleton. The victim told several arguments why his life should be spared, but these are found insufficient and death, accompanied by an entourage of other skeletal figures, takes the victim away.

Dance of Death in the German printed edition, folio CCLXI recto from Hartman Schedel's Chronicle of the World (Nuremberg, 1493).

Danse Macabre, art by Hans Holbein, 1491.

Death as a Tarot Card

For centuries, a popular source of amusement and fortune telling was the Tarot. This series of cards would outline ones future or answer a question one might have by laying out the mixed cards in a particular order. The Death card has been know to frequently depict a skeleton riding a horse, surrounded by dead and dying people from all classes in much the same way as *La Danse Macabre*. The skeleton carries a black standard emblazoned with a white flower and, according to the Rider-Waite deck, symbolizes rebirth. It really is an indication of an end, possibly of a relationship, but does not necessarily foretell of death itself. However the resemblance and meaning are still profound.

The Masque of the Red Death

Originally published as *The Mask of the Red Death* in 1842 by Edgar Allen Poe, the story follows Prince Prospero's attempts to avoid an epidemic called The Red Death. As he entertains his wealthy friends, a mysterious figure enters and makes his way through the abbey. This disease was one of agony and the victim was said, in the story, to sweat blood instead of perspiration. Prospero and his friends felt safe in their fortress and reacted callously to the sufferings of the commoners outside. They intended to wait out the plague in luxury and safety behind the walls of his refuge.

At midnight, Prospero notices one figure in a blood-spattered, dark robe with a skull-like mask depicting a victim of the Red Death. Prospero demands to know the identity of the mysterious guest so that they can hang him, and when none obey, pursues him with a drawn dagger. When at last Prospero confronts this stranger, the figure turns to face him, and the Prince falls dead at a glance. The gathered guests swarm into the black room and remove the mask, only to find both it and the robes empty.

The story is an allegory, and the figure reveals itself as the personification of Death itself, and all the guests succumb to the disease. The final line of the story is, "And Darkness and Decay and the Red Death held illimitable dominion over all." Horror master Vincent Price played in the film adaptation by the same name.

CHARON

Charon herds sinners onto his boat, Alighieri Gustave Dore Dante, 1857.

In Roman mythology, Pluto is the god of the underworld, and Charon is the ferryman across the river Styx, the moat into Pluto's realm. Hermes would bring to Charon the souls of the deceased, and he would ferry them across the river to Hades. Charon was a somber and harsh figure, did not hesitate to throw out of his boat, without pity, the souls whose bodies received improper burial or who were without coin to pay him, which is why, in ancient Greek burial rites, the corpse always had a silver coin, or obolus, placed under their tongue. Charon is depicted frequently in art of the fifth and fourth centuries B.C. with scenes of the dead boarding his boat. In the first century B.C. the poet Virgil describes Charon in the course *Descent into the Underworld.*

> There Chairon stands, who rules the dreary coast—
> A sordid god: down from his hairy chin
> A length of beard descends, uncombed, unclean;
> His eyes, like hollow furnaces on fire;
> A girdle, foul with grease, binds his obscene attire.

Charon also has appeared as a shaggy and thin old man or sometimes, in later art, as a winged demon wielding a double hammer. His demeanor was sullen and fierce, no matter his look.

The Styx is only one of the five rivers of the underworld that separate Hades from the world of the living. The word *styx* comes from the Greek word *stugein,* which means hateful and represents the horror of death. Ancient beliefs held that the Styx water was poisonous.

The use of the figures of Charon and the River Styx is quite recurrent in Western literature, such as found in the thirteenth century, when the Italian poet, Dante Alighien, used Charon in his famous *Divine Comedy*, in which Charon sees a living man and Dante's alter ego, journeying into the depths of the inferno and challenges him. The classic artist Michelangelo's interpretation was in turn influenced by Dante's and shows him with an oar over his shoulder.

Symbolism of the Grim Reaper

Everything about the Grim Reaper is filled with meaning and is a symbol associated with death. From the objects he carries to the death shroud he wears, they all tell us something about his nature and symbolism. The skeletal figure represents the decay of the flesh, and serves to reinforce one of our biggest fears, that of being forgotten. The black cloak, or death shroud, is one of the most common things associated with the figure of death. Black has long been linked with death and mourning. But typically black is the color of evil forces and power. The black cloak serves as a means to give the Reaper an air of mystery and menace, and is worn by figures like Darth Vader and Batman. The things we can't see frighten us as much as the things we can see, so the shadows under the hooded cloak reach us deeply as they tap into our fears of the unknown. I recall seeing an old movie of *Scrooge* as a young child and the last ghost depicted as the reaper scared, yet fascinated me!

In early depictions, the Reaper is shown holding arrows or spears, weapons he uses to strike down his victim but the most prominent symbol is that of the scythe. A scythe was a tool used to reap, or cut, grain or grass. As people harvest crops in the fall, death harvests peoples' lives. Sometimes the Reaper carries an hour glass. This classic timepiece has two glass bulbs containing sand that takes an hour to pour from one end to another, and as such has itself become a symbol for time; an hour glass indicating symbolically that when the sand runs out, our time is up. The *Bible's* Book of Revelation talks of four horsemen, Pestilence, War, Famine and Death, that appear signaling the end of the world. Death rides a pale horse, which is often interpreted as pale green, the color of disease and decay. The Man in Black, singer Johnny Cash, sang about a pale horse in several songs, and was famous for his legacy of melancholy and redemption, living on as a Reaper in music to many.

The Grim Reaper also plays a key role in many famous creations, such as the 1957 film *The Seventh Seal* which tells of a knight who returns from the Crusades to find that the plague has killed many of his countrymen. *Because I Could Not Stop for Death,* a poem by Emily Dickinson, in which the narrator shares a carriage ride with Death, *(Don't Fear) The Reaper*, a song released by Blue Öyster Cult in 1976, and "Death" itself is the name of a comic book character, who appears as a girl, by Neil Gamien in his most popular work *Sandman*. Brad Pitt starred in the role of Death in a 1998 film titled *Meet Joe Black*, a remake of a 1934 film titled *Death Takes a Holiday*. This remake that depicts Death's decision to see what it's like to be mortal. In a Showtime television series called *Dead Like Me*, starring actor Mandy Patinkin, we explores the lives and afterlives of a group of grim reapers who walk among the living.

Killing Edge, Spiral USA clothing art graphic.

Sand of souls Spiral USA, clothing art graphic.

Grim Reaper ashtray.

Grim Reaper, oil painting by author, 2009.

October issue cover photo, *Courtesy Dark Gothic Resurrected Magazine, 2009.*

Opposite:
Death Comes for Me, graphic art by Drake Mefestta, *Courtesy Ticia Martyr Image Photography, 2010.*

SKULLS

Skulls have been given strong religious meanings in many cultures, such as in the Hindu culture, where skull beads are used in a necklace as an iconographic reminder, and are decorations, worn by certain gods and goddesses, such as Shiva and Kali. The skull and crossbones, as a symbol, is also used in initiation rituals as a symbol of rebirth and the promise of a new life. Many cultures saw the skull as a form of liberation from life's troubles. Even Christianity used a skull at the bottom of the crucifix, representing Adam's burial in order to have the blood wash away man's sins.

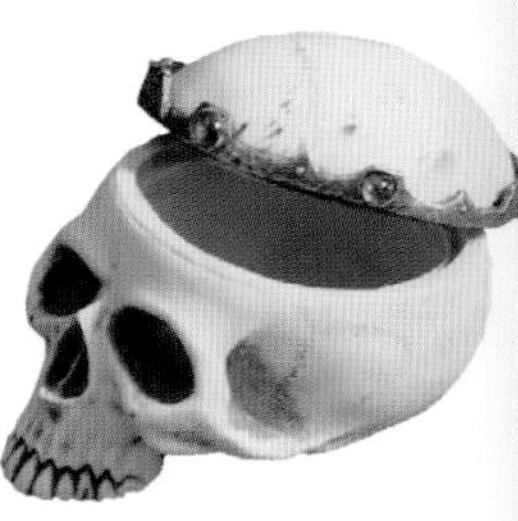

Skull stash box, *Courtesy of Alchemy Gothic, 2010.*

Skull ring, *Courtesy of Alchemy Gothic, 2010.*

Hourglass of the dead, graphic art by Drake Mefestta, *Courtesy Ticia Martyr Image Photography, 2010.*

Skull cups, used in Tibetan Rituals, are traditionally formed from the oval upper section of a human cranium that has been cut into shape, lined with a metal rim and elaborately decorated with Buddhist symbols like lotuses. Skull cups are used primarily in Tibetan rituals and symbolic art, but also as the begging bowl when used as a constant reminder of death and impermanence.

When used for esoteric rituals, the history of the skull's original owner has a powerful effect to the believer in its potency. The skull of a murder or execution victim is believed to possess the greatest tantric power; the skull of one who has died from a violent or accidental death, this force, or potential, of the skull's previous owner is thought to be contained within the bone making it a prized tool in performance of rituals. Lord Byron, the great Romantic poet during the time of the writing of the classic story of Frankenstein (indeed Byron and the horror author Mary Shelly were good friends) was said to have a skull goblet crafted from the abbey on his property and he used it often during wild chaotic parties he was famous for.

Skull goblet, *Courtesy Alchemy Gothic, 2010.*

Lord George Gordon Byron, 1800s, artist unknown.

MAY BE CREEPY ... BUT TRUE

A replica of the skull goblet crafted from Byron's Abbey is sold by Alchemy Gothic—they have a fine reproduction of this, having a heavy resin realistic skull and solid pewter base. (I had the pleasure of getting one recently myself.)

In Freemasonry, the skull and crossbones, or a crossed hoe and scepter, are symbols of sovereignty. A skull above important emblems is used to symbolize a hierarchic structure and evolution of the material world. Many Presidents, doctors, and lawyers have been members of this order (including my great grandfather and grandfather).

Skulls were often engraved or carved on tombstones as a symbol of mortality, and death's head skulls have long been the mark we associate with secret societies, such as The Skull and Bones Society, to label poisons, and appeared on black-flagged pirate ships, called a Jolly Roger.

Well through the nineteenth century, the Grim Reaper was found on headstones as the winged death's heads seen on Colonial graves. Often one can see carvings of skulls used to decorate doorways and hallways of ancient ceremonial grounds and sanctuaries.

Crossroads

In many cultures, the crossroads is a location between the worlds where two realms meet, where one can exchange their soul for extraordinary gifts or fame. The selling-your-soul-to-the-Devil-for-power story has become a staple in many songs, and made famous in *The Devil Went Down To Georgia.*

Historically, burial at a crossroads formed a crude cross and this gave rise to the belief that these spots were selected as the next best burying places to consecrated ground. Necromancers who did rituals and were said to command the dead performed ghastly deeds at crossroads dressed in dead people's clothing. There is also the custom of burying criminals at crossroad, and more than likely due to the fact it was a symbolic marking of the desire to bury those outside of the law outside the city, thus keeping the evil away. Suicides were buried at crossroads during the night because of the superstition folklore told tales of the dead capable of coming back as vampires. They felt the cross shape of the crossroads would inhibit their ability to return.

Not only was the ferryman, Charon, attributed to carrying the dead from one life to the next, so were birds of other cultures.

Ravens

The raven has been a powerful symbol and a popular subject of mythology and folklore across time and in every nation it existed in. The most famous student of psychologist Sigmund Freud was Carl Jung, who declared the Shadow or the dark side of the psyche, was the repressed parts of our feelings. He deemed the raven to symbolize or represent the shadow self. Our deepest shadow is the fear of our own end and makes sense of why symbols such as The Reaper and dark birds loom in our collective minds as things that frighten us.

Crow, graphic image shirt art, Spiral USA, 2010.

Ravens and crows have many myths surrounding them, which I will explain in depth. Ravens belong to the family of birds called corvidae. Surprisingly, I found that ravens hold funerals for their dead. One bird will guard the body and rasp out a death song, as others form a circle around the corpse. They then hop in a dance round and round, croaking. As we will find, a great number of myths and ancient religions recognize the Raven as a harbinger of death. To the ancient Celtics, the raven was one of the most important symbols of death because they were scavengers that consumed corpses on the battlefield. Warriors would find ravens eating the flesh of the fallen, thus adding to their mystique as guardian spirit of the dead.

Europeans associated the raven with war, death, and spirits of the dead. Much to my surprise however, I found the Raven has not always been strictly associated with darkness. These stories speak of the wisdom and ingenuity, as in the case of the ancient Greeks, who used the terms for "crow" and "raven" interchangeably. Corvus, the Crow, is allied with Apollo, whose chariot across the sky explained the suns travel. The story goes that the raven, who was colored white at that time, took flight for the gods and was too close to the heat of the sun, scorching his wings black.

In Norse mythology, the ruler of the gods, known as Odin, had a pair of ravens named Hugin, meaning thought, and Munin, meaning remembrance, that would perch on his shoulder or throne. Every morning they flew around the earth observing everything and asking questions of everyone, including the dead. Returning by nightfall to their master, they whispered all that they had discovered to him.

The Celtic goddess Morrigan, was also accompanied by three ravens, named Babd, Acha and Neman, which were the three goddess of war and were eaters of carrion. As such they served as messengers of death, pestilence, and battle. It was believed that these flesh-hungry birds could smell the scent of death upon a person before they died.

In paintings, and even on the cover of videos at your local rental store, the raven may be seen flying over battlefields, haunted houses, or in the ominous skies of horror movies, waiting for the dead. They are featured in everything from Edgar Allan Poe's classic turned into movies or as a part of the film itself in *Resident Evil's* third installment, *Extinction*, where they were infected with the zombie virus.

Kwahwumhl, Native raven art, artist unknown, *Courtesy Library of Congress.*

May Be Creepy ... But True

Even the *Bible* talks about ravens in hordes descending on the nations of the Earth, devouring the wicked after Revelations. There have been stories written about them plucking out the eyes of hanged criminals.

In many Western traditions, ravens have long been considered to be birds of bad omens, and were the symbol of sins such as gluttony and theft. Christians have long held the thought that ravens or crows carried off the souls of the damned and associated this bird with Satan, in part because they believed it was the antithesis of a white dove. Conversely, for some aboriginal traditions, this bird is a beneficent guide that issues warnings to the living and to lead the dead on their final journey. According to several traditions from Native American tribes, stories of the raven say he stole the moon and sun from the Great Spirit (or God) and put them in the sky for humans. Native Americans believe the raven was a bearer of magic, and messenger of the spirit world. In many cultures and times, the belief is held that these birds are messengers of the Spirit Realm. The story of the crow as the carrier of the dead soul was the basis for James O'Barr's famous comic book turned movie series, *The Crow*.

The most well known literary influence on the subject of death is described by Edgar Allan Poe in his uncannily beautiful poem, *The Raven*. It talks of a man, distraught with grief, mourning the loss of his beloved, who hears a rapping at the door. Opening the study door to peer into darkness he whispers the name of his beloved Lenore. In the classic Poe style, the first person narrative of an insane person, the man seems to believe that somehow she has returned from the dead. He again hears that sound, this time from the window. Flinging open the window a Raven flies in, landing on a bust of Pallas above the door. Pallas Athene, pagan goddess of wisdom, is very symbolic in this poem due to the fact she represents human reason, and the arts. Drawing on more classic Greek and Roman influences, the man calls out to the Raven as having come from the "Night's Plutonian shore." Pluto, another deity discussed in earlier chapters, was lord of the realm of the dead. When the man begs a name of his visitor, the bird responds with only a single word, "Nevermore."

Countless cultures point to the raven as a messenger of powerful knowledge, secrets and the winged transporter for the souls of the dead.

Edgar Allan Poe book cover *Nevermore, Courtesy of Dark Moon Press 2010.*

Raven Poe shirt graphic, *Courtesy of Alchemy Gothic, 2010.*

The Raven, poetry illustration, date and artist unknown.

Poe watch, *Courtesy of Alchemy Gothic, 2010.*

Poe necklace, *Courtesy of Alchemy Gothic, 2010.*

Chapter Four

Momento Mori

"Remember man as you pass by. As you are now so once was I: As I am now so you must be! Prepare for death and follow me."

~ Memento Mori inscription from a gravestone in New Jersey

A Momento Mori is a form of image that urged a European person of the late Middle Ages to, as it translates, "remember thy death." To do this, a memento mori might represent death as a human skeleton—perhaps as the Grim Reaper gathering his harvest—or it might depict human bodies in an advanced state of decay.

Victorian Mourning Customs

Victorian Mourning Customs from *Collier's Encyclopedia*, published in 1901, detailed a great amount of mourning customs. From jewelry, clothing, to mementos made of hair, Victorians extended their bereavement into almost every aspect of their lives.

Today the word "Victorian" refers to a certain highly ornate style of architecture, furnishings, and fashion. It is a style that most people of the Gothic persuasion look to with romantic longing, which we'll look at in the last chapter. The nineteenth-century cemeteries that cover most of America today are the most visible and recognizable symbol of this bygone era. Primarily, the one element of Victorian style that continues to endure and fascinate us is the mourning fashions of the day.

The Victorian age was named for England's Queen Victoria. Mourning, as a fad, reached its height after the death of Prince Albert in December 1861. Queen Victoria ordered that his room remain precisely as it was at the time of his death. Her longing for her late husband led her to sleep with a photo of him that was taken at the time of the showing of his body. Any of the family photos taken after Prince Albert's death also included a life size marble bust of him in the center of the group. Queen Victoria required everyone at court to wear mourning attire on social occasions for three years, and she herself wore nothing but black and remained a semi-recluse until she died on January 22, 1901. Her deep mourning was imitated by her countrymen when dealing with their own losses, and trickled into America as well.

Into the nineteenth century, death hovered over everyone as a daily possibility, and it grew more and more. As Victorian society was bound and structured by elaborate rules of etiquette, these rules gave order to a society that changed rapidly as the Industrial Revolution created the middle class. Etiquette books instructed the newly wealthy in the details of socially acceptable behavior. One of the areas of life that had a very strict social code was, quite ironically about death.

Victorian Mourning, graphic art by Drake Mefestta, ***Courtesy Ticia Martyr Image Photography, 2010.***

Draping the studio, Courtesy Library of Congress.

Covered Mirrors

During the Victorian Era many superstitions still remained, and especially those concerning death. When there was a corpse in the house it was believed to be necessity to cover all the mirrors in order to keep the deceased's spirit from becoming trapped within. They also believed if a mirror in a home was to fall and break by itself, it meant that someone in the home would soon die. When someone died in the house and there was a clock in the room, the clock had to be stopped at the death hour or the family of the household would have bad luck. When the body was taken from the house, it had to be carried out feet first because if it was carried out head first, it could look back and beckon others to follow it into death.

Fashion

Victorian mourning fashion was aimed mainly at women, widows in particular. For the first year, a woman who was in mourning was not allowed to exit her home without full black attire and a weeping veil. Her activities were initially restricted to church services. Mourning attire was the perfect way to show the wealth and respectability of a woman. Some went so far as to dress their servants for mourning when the head of the household passed away. Middle and lower-class women would go to great lengths to appear fashionable in times of mourning. Dying clothing black and then bleaching them out again was quite common.

May be Creepy ... But True

The industry of mourning became so vital to tailors that rumors were spread concerning the bad luck of recycling funeral attire.

Mourning had two stages: deep, or full, mourning and half-mourning. Each stage had its own rules and customs of decorum.

Deep Mourning

When someone died, all the members of the household (including the servants) would adopt deep mourning. Curtains were drawn and clocks were stopped at the time of death. Mirrors were covered. The body was watched over every moment until burial. The prevalence of grave robbers prompted many to hire guards to watch over the grave.

Funerals could not be too elaborate. Coffins were intricately carved and decorated with gilding. Hearses and the horses that pulled them were adorned with black ostrich plumes. Sometimes the horses were actually dyed black and fitted with black and silver trappings. Professional mourners called mutes would be hired to walk in the funeral procession and lavish refreshments were served after interment, in much the same manner as Irish wakes. Funerals for children featured white accents: white gloves on the mourners, white ostrich plumes on the horses, a white coffin for the child.

Deep mourning demanded that women adopt a wardrobe made entirely of black crepe, a dull fabric without any sheen to reflect light. Even parasols and handkerchiefs were trimmed in black, without decoration. Men wore plain black suits with black armbands. Children also wore black, and even babies were dressed in white garments trimmed with black ribbons.

Specific periods of time were considered appropriate for mourning. A widow was bound to adhere to these customs more than a widower, and was expected to mourn her husband for at least two years more. Such customs involved wearing heavy, concealing, black costume and the use of black crepe veils. Special black caps and bonnets were worn with these ensembles. Widows were expected to wear these clothes up to four years after their loss to show their grief. Jewelry was generally not worn the first year.

Half Mourning

After one year of deep mourning, a widow progressed to half-mourning, and could trade her black crepe dress for a silk one. Half-mourning allowed for jewelry made of pearls, amethysts, black cut glass, and jet. A popular trend was to incorporate a lock of the deceased's hair into mourning jewelry. After a year of half-mourning, a widow could freely wear any color, although many followed the lead of Queen Victoria and remained in black for the rest of their lives.

No other relation was mourned quite so long as a spouse. Parents who lost a child wore deep mourning for nine months and half-mourning for three. Children mourned deceased parents for a similar length of time. The death of a sibling required three months of deep mourning and three months of half-mourning. The deaths of in-laws, aunts and uncles, cousins, and other relatives each demanded some degree of public mourning, ranging from six weeks to three months. It was not unusual for an individual to spend the better part of a year dressed in mourning for one departed relative after another. Half mourning lasted from three to six months and was represented by more elaborate fabrics used as trim. Gradually easing back into color was expected coming out of half mourning. All manner of jewelry could be worn.

The standard mourning time for a widower was two years but it was up to his discretion when to end his single stage. Men could go about their daily lives and continue to work. Typically, young unmarried men stayed in mourning for as long as the women in the household did.

Death infiltrated many objects in the nineteenth century, quite apart from clothing. Throughout the period, certain images were used again and again to represent the frailty and the brevity of human life. Draped urns, broken columns, weeping willows, and extinguished torches can be spotted in articles as diverse as tombstones, portraits, children's books, and embroidered samplers. The same imagery even recurs in the literature and poetry of the day. Bereavement touched virtually every aspect of Victorian life, lending a somber hue to even the brightest day.

Most of the fabrics associated with Victorian life are no longer in use today, partially due to the invention of modern synthetic fabrics, but also because many Victorian fabrics are too expensive to manufacture today. A full widow's weeds (archaic word for garment) in the mid-nineteenth century required a crepe dress with a plain collar and broad weeper's cuffs made of white muslin, a bombazine mantle (cloak), and a crepe bonnet with veil for outdoors. A widow's cap was for indoor use. Crepe, used for the veil and trim, is the fabric most associated with mourning. The fabric is made from silk and similar to crepe de chine; in this instance "crepe" refers to the crinkled surface of the lightweight fabric. Mourning crepe was made from gummed, tightly twisted silk threads. It was a volatile and hazardous fabric. In the rain, it would shrivel and practically disintegrate. Rain-proof crepe was introduced at the turn of the twentieth century, but it didn't change things much. Constant breathing through the fabric caused many respiratory health problems.

Dresses were often made from crepe. As the crepe wore out, it was removed and replaced with fresh material. An economical woman could use an old dress in full mourning; some women dyed a dress black for this purpose.

Mourning attire by designer Kambriel Fashions, *Courtesy of Kambriel, 2010.*

Mourning attire Men's frock coat by designer Kambriel Fashions, *Courtesy of Kambriel, 2010.*

Opposite:
Mourning attire bustle by designer Kambriel Fashions, *Courtesy of Kambriel, 2010.*

Mourning attire by designer Kambriel Fashions, *Courtesy of Kambriel, 2010.*

Mourning attire by designer Kambriel Fashions, *Courtesy of Kambriel, 2010.*

Colors

The color black best represented the Victorian act of mourning because it symbolized the absence of light and in turn, life. It was an instantly recognizable sign that a loved one had departed this life.

May Be Creepy ... But True

It has been said that wearing black for mourning comes from a Roman idea; the mourners could prevent being haunted from the ghost of the deceased by cloaking themselves in black.

Black was not the only color that signaled mourning. In full mourning, white was used for cuffs and collars. By half mourning, a woman had a bevy of colors to choose from, by comparison. Grey, mauve, purple, lavender, lilac, and white could all be implemented. Deep reds such as burgundy were also fashionable in the late Victorian era. Subtle prints using any combination of these colors were also allowed. This trend was more popular in the south because of the weather. Dressing in full white, including the weeping veil, was a sign of mourning in the tropics.

Children's attire was white with black trim in the summer and gray with black trim in the winter. This was mostly for infants and young girls. Children under the age of 15 were thought not to be able to handle the grief brought on by assuming mourning. A girl was considered a woman at 17 and could be in full mourning if a loved one was to die.

Jewelry

At the same time as the Queen's deep depression, over in the United States, the use of mourning jewelry and attire increased with the outbreak of the Civil War. Mourning jewelry was a souvenir to remember a loved one, a reminder to the living of the inevitability of death, and a status symbol, especially during the Victorian era that mirrored the times of the people who wore it.

The earliest examples of mourning jewelry were found in Europe in the fifteenth century in the form of black and white enameled heads or skulls that were set into rings for men and brooches for women. Later on in the seventeenth and eighteenth centuries, it was a status symbol to receive mourning rings from the bereaved family to friends and other family members as a memorial to the deceased. The wealthy often gave instructions in their wills as to how the jewelry was to look, a form of a memorial for themselves. White enamel was used for the death of a single person and black enamel for a married person. Much the same as on tombstones, the deceased person's name, dates of birth and death were inscribed around the ring, as well as symbols of death such as coffins, serpents or miniatures of those mourned were set in the ring. One of the earliest known rings was from the 1600s and showed a portrait of Charles I on one side and a skull and a crown on the other. The inscription read, *The glory of England has departed.* The Death's Head symbol is still used often today, by companies such as Alchemy Gothic, on jewelry modeled after old mourning rings.

Alchemy Gothic Cemetery Cross, *Courtesy Alchemy 2010.*

Although enamel was used in mourning rings, jet had been used for mourning for thousands of years. This hard black material is formed when soaked driftwood becomes embedded in the mud on the bottom of the ocean floor. Like diamonds, a combination of heat and pressure causes the material to be transformed into a compact black substance that is quite fragile. It is found throughout the world and easily carved. Examples have been found in caves from prehistoric times. Early superstition has it that the shiny surface deflected the evil away from the person wearing it, and during the Middle Ages in Europe it is not surprising that it became one of the most common substances used in mourning jewelry.

Queen Victoria decreed that only jet jewelry was to be worn at court for the first year of mourning. By the 1850s, there were fifty jet workshops in Whitby alone, which increased in twenty years to two hundred. Jet was used for brooches, bracelets, and necklaces. This lead to a shortage of jet which caused many imitations to began to appear. Onyx and black glass became a huge export from the United States in 1893, used mainly for beads and small items.

Hair Jewelry

Hair was long considered a symbol of life, but also associated with death and funerals in many cultures. Egyptian tomb paintings portray scenes showing royalty gifting each other with hair balls as love offerings. Hair jewelry began in the United States during the Civil War, as the soldiers would leave a lock of hair with their families. Upon the soldier's death, this was often made into a piece of jewelry or placed in a locket, engraved with "In Memory Of" and the name of the deceased. A few museums where hair work is displayed are the Dearborn Historical Society and the Henry Ford Museum.

The fashion for all mourning jewelry came to an end at the turn of the twentieth century with the death of Queen Victoria and the beginning of the First World War.

Embalming During the Civil War

Dr. Thomas Holmes, the son of a wealthy merchant, made a reputation for himself during the Civil War as he went from one battlefield to the next, where he charged $7 per enlisted man and $13 per peer officer to perform the embalming process. He began by draping the operating tent in black cloth for privacy. He used a makeshift table made from two whiskey barrels and an old door, and several bottles of fluid that was forced into the body by means of a hose and rubber ball that was squeezed to create a pump. This process would take hours and later the remains were shipped in a coffin to the family of the deceased.

Inside a second tent, alongside his portable lodgings, was a desk with family pictures, toiletries, a bible and a pistol where he would record any available information on his work, such as the soldier's name, address, rank, unit and date of embalming. Dr. Holmes experimented with pharmacy compounds and developed his own blend of embalming fluid that he sold to surgeons and undertakers. His fame rose to new heights in the Washington papers when he performed this process on a security guard of President Lincoln.

Mourning Photography

There was also a common custom, although it seems odd today, that consisted of having photographs taken of the dead. Perhaps it was another trend started by Queen Victoria, we cannot be sure. It was not uncommon to see photographs with people seated around a relative's tombstone, and sometimes the dead were posed as part of family groups, as you can see in the movie *The Haunting in Connecticut*, which featured in the opening credits post-mortem photos.

Some of these photos featured the person lying down, appearing asleep in their death bed, or laying in their casket. In others, the person was propped up, dressed in their normal attire or finest clothing. Many images can be found with eyes painted onto their eyelids or inked in after the photo was taken. In most cases, the only way you can be sure which person is dead is by paying close attention to the fact that the face is very clear because with the long exposure times needed to gain enough light for proper exposure, the living people tended to be blurred because of fidgeting. In some cases, especially with very young children, there might well have been no other photographs for the family to remember them by. Back in the early days of photography, as with all new technology, such mementos were expensive, so most people didn't have them done frequently.

The End of an Era

In 1901, the Victorian era ended, giving way to the Edwardian era, and it was as if the world came out of mourning. Fashion changed slowly. During The Civil War, half a million soldiers died. With nearly the whole population in mourning it caused a greater depression which lead to an attempt to pass a law banning Victorian mourning fashion due to the low morale of the populace. Other facets of people's lives quickly evolved, technology increased, and "the War to end all Wars" brought women into the workplace and gave them better things to do than dress in mourning. Industry had taken over and people lived in a more modern and efficient society. The romantic relationship with life and death, that so appeals to the Gothic subculture, was all but gone.

Museums of Death

Museum of Mourning

The Museum of Mourning Photography and Memorial Practice was founded by Anthony R. Vizzari and is operated by A&A Studios, Inc. This museum owns and protects over a thousand mourning photographs and negatives, from about 1840 to present. In addition to photography, there is also an archive of writings. Presently, the collection may only be viewed by limited appointment and is located in Oak Park, Illinois.

Camden County Historical Society's Fall Festival program which focused on nineteenth-century cemetery architecture and mourning customs was as enjoyable as it was educational. The Society's headquarters in Parkside is near a heavily wooded grounds of the 170-year-old Harleigh. Visitors are taken on tour by Harleigh manager Chris Mojica and the operations manager Donna DiFiore, both dressed in the period costume of 1880s funeral directors.

In several countries in Western Europe, a variety of museums, such as the Funeral Museum in Vienna, Austria, as well as the Museum for Sepulchral Culture in Kassel, Germany, are dedicated exclusively to death, dying, and remembrance. This seems to be indicative of a slowly changing attitude toward death. These museums exist as a way to preserve culture of funeral history and pictorial documents of these events, and delicately take into consideration our sensitivity to the subject when displaying these curiosities. Founded in 1967 as a branch of the Vienna Municipal Funeral Department, the Vienna Funeral Museum focuses primarily on displaying the history of the company with pictures, documents, coffins, urns, funeral coaches, and more. This museum became the model for a similarly organized museum, The Museum of Piety in Budapest, Hungary, which opened in 1991.

The "Museum fuer Sepulkralkultur," which means *The Museum of Sepulchral Culture in Kassel,* is supported by The Association for Cemetery and Memorial, and was built completely with public funds. However, daily needs are mostly paid by the government, the municipality, and churches. Its primary goal is to promote public understanding of the culture of funerals, cemeteries, and mourning with exhibits that focus on various aspects of Germany's cultural history of funerals, trends, and artists' rendering reflecting on dying and mourning. There are also cemetery museums in Switzerland, and The National Funeral Museum located in London, created by an undertaker from London's West End, with an impressive collection of both historical horse drawn hearses as well as one of the oldest motorized funeral coaches, historical funeral equipment, old drawings and prints, shrouds, mourning dresses, and mourning jewelry. In addition, an extensive library was founded. The Netherlands has the Museum of Exit, is still under construction.

Lincoln's funeral procession, *Courtesy Library of Congress.*

A History of Hearses

In the funeral industry, a hearse isn't usually called a hearse; instead, they refer to it as a funeral coach. This comes from the fact that in history, horse-drawn coaches were used to carry coffins to the cemetery, and remains in use today. The word "hearse" actually comes from the Middle English "herse," which referred to a type of candelabra often placed on top of a coffin. During the seventeenth century, people started using the word to refer to the horse-drawn carriages that conveyed the casket to the place of burial during a funeral procession, depending on a person's social class. In the mid 1800s, with the establishment of funeral parlors and funeral homes, the funeral director created a lengthy service for the deceased's survivors, and the undertaker's carriage that transported the deceased, with mourners following on foot at first, and later in carriages.

A further sign of the deceased's wealth included the plume, the large feather that was attached to the top of the carriage and to the horses' heads as well. The poor person did not have plumes, and two plumes represented the middle class. The higher the number, the better off the deceased was, with the wealthiest of funeral clients, who may have displayed seven plumes or more.

Lincolns hearse, *Courtesy Library of Congress.*

Arch at Twelfth Street, Lincoln's funeral, *Courtesy Library of Congress.*

Hearses remained horse-drawn until the first decade of the twentieth century, when motorized hearses began to appear. Between 1901 and 1907, the first electric-powered hearses were built. Then, in 1909, the first gas-powered engine was used for the funeral of Wilfrid A. Pruyn. This vehicle was built from the body of a horse-drawn hearse and a bus chassis. This new type of hearse, quite popular with the funeral home's wealthier patrons, cost about $6,000 per hearse, whereas a horse-drawn hearse of that time was only $1,500. It was too expensive for most funeral homes to afford the newer method. After some time however, combustion engines became more powerful and cheaper, and funeral directors realized that automobiles would mean more funerals per day, and motorized hearses became the standard by the 1920s.

The first manufacturer of hearses was Crane and Breed Company in Cincinnati, Ohio, and other companies soon began building them as well. By the 1930s the longer sleek classic-style hearse was introduced by Sayers and Scovill, has only slightly been modified today. In the early twentieth-century hearses were both funeral coaches and ambulances. These were

PEACE NOBLE SOUL, PATRIOT
Faithful to Right, A Martyr to Justice

termed "combination coaches," depending on the immediate need that the community had for them. For obvious health reasons, it was done away with around the 1970s.

The collecting of hearses has caught on with thousands of automobile enthusiasts, as many people enjoy the look of classic hearses so much they collect and restore them. I have several friends who own them. They talk about their love for the macabre—some are decked out with skeletons or wildly creepy but beautiful paint jobs—or, as most Goths do, about their fondness of a time when most cars were large, luxurious and even handcrafted.

The rare horse-drawn hearses were shown on a recent television show where two gentlemen use them as transport to search for antiques to possibly restore and resell. There was an elderly man who owned a half dozen of these beautiful hearses all the way up to the much sought after Cadillac and Packard hearses from the '50 and '60s, especially the 1959 Cadillac hearses, that had huge fins. The major drawback a friend of mine in Chicago told me is that, due to the weight the vehicle carries, they are built on a much heavier chassis and as such are not very economical when it comes to fuel consumption.

The Phantom Coaches Hearse Club was formed in the spring of 1994, consisting of almost 200 members. Members attend monthly meetings at various locations and they also publish a monthly club newsletter for their members, called *The Epitaph*. As unusual as they may seem, it is not a rare thing. The Professional Car Society was formed to bring attention to these vehicles and remind us what a treasure

11792S

Horse drawn hearses in front of funeral parlor, *Courtesy of Library of Congress, 1908.*

they offer us to observe, as much as the original Model T is to the average car collector, they too have a place in history. Gregg D. Merksamer, author *of Professional Cars: Ambulances, Hearses and Flower Cars,* suggests that the society was able to overcome the stigma surrounding hearses by forbidding any display of caskets, skulls or other spooky artifacts at auto shows and club functions, emphasizing instead what wonderful pieces of automotive memorabilia these vehicles truly are. Along with several friends, Bryan Moore, a notable sculptor and filmmaker, coordinated the 2005 World's Longest Hearse Procession at the Petersen Automotive Museum in Los Angeles, California, where the record was set at seventy-six hearses, as well as curating the only hearse exhibit ever held at the same museum. Phantom Hearses is run by Mr. Moore. He is a Priest in the Church of Satan and has represented this group many times in the media, including appearances on The History Channel, *Fox News*, CBS, NBC, ABC, *20/20* and many others. Mr. Moore has, for many years, been an avid collector of classic Cadillacs and hearses, including the 1951 hearse used in Ed Wood's film.

In Costa Mesa, there is an annual hearse show begun by Clarence Williams of Santa Ana, who helped get the Phantom Coaches with Robert Dean of Orange, California. Both gentlemen coordinate the event and enjoy driving their hearses at other times in the year. Hearse Club in Englewood, Colorado even displayed a hearse based off the *A-Team,* and HearseCon has been featured on the Travel Channel, national news, the Syndicated Press and *Rebel Rodz Magazine*. In addition to the Professional Car Society, organizations like the National Hearse and Ambulance Association and the Last Ride Hearse Society have sprung up, as well as groups like the Denver Hearse Association, the Tomb, Grim Rides, Dark Ends, Last Ryds and more can be found all over the United States. Canada has a hearse club as well; Black Widow Hearse Club is based out of Ontario. The club officially came to be on February 20th, 2008, but came up with the idea just after Halloween of 2007. Begun by Darren, Don, and Wayne, they decided to create a club to promote the love for these types of vehicles. Their mission statement is, "Have fun before we all die."

As the website for Black Widow Hearse Club says, "*let's face it, we're here to enjoy these amazing vehicles before we end up in the back of one, or they end up in the junk yard. So we're going to do our best to give you as many opportunities as possible to enjoy them yourself.*"

I couldn't say it better myself.

JP Morgan hearse, *Courtesy Library of Congress.*

Morgan Hearse leaving St. Georges, *Courtesy Library of Congress.*

Jefferson Davis funeral car, *Courtesy Library of Congress.*

Admiral Schley hearse, *Courtesy Library of Congress.*

1923 Hearse outside library of congress, *Courtesy Library of Congress.*

Early Ford hearse, *Courtesy Library of Congress.*

Funeral car, Havana, Cuba, *Courtesy Library of Congress.*

Lincoln memorial wreaths, *Courtesy Library of Congress.*

Chapter Five

THE THRESHOLD BETWEEN

"Death is a Dialogue between, the Spirit and the Dust."
~ Emily Dickinson (1830-1886)
American Poet

In the past it was common for people to attempt to receive communications from the dead, and whether or not we give this serious validity in this day and age or not, perhaps it helps people through their grief process. Famous psychics today, such as Sylvia Brown, help clients all over as they seek comfort in hearing how their loved ones feel about them, forgive them, or a myriad of other things they need to know to find closure. The messages conveyed are that the person is not truly gone, merely somewhere else, a happier and healthier place for them. Other writers have similar beliefs, Linda Georgian, nationally known psychic and author of *Your Guardian Angels*, talks about how to reach beyond the limits of your five senses to contact the departed. *Transitions of the Soul* and *Visitations From the Afterlife* are both filled with a collection of stories from people retelling their stories of communications with deceased friends and family.

But do spirits really linger on after death, one often asks. From my own thoughts, thus far there is little hard evidence of conscious survival after death. I do not rule out that there might be some form of non-conscious residue left which could have been created by people in dire emotional states which sensitive individuals might perceive after the death of said person. I feel we should keep our minds open, remaining skeptical but not dismissing the possibility. If something exists, then it should be demonstrable, recordable and repeatable, as I mentioned on my first television consultation for A&E's show *Paranormal State* for the episode *Satan's Solider*.

Spirits of the dead have been called upon in recorded history in a great many ancient books, from *Ulysses* to the *Bible* when The Witch of Endor was consulted by King Saul to predict the outcome of a great battle. King Saul was terribly afraid in doing so because he was familiar with the passage "There shall not be found among you [any one] that

Original Ouija board, *Courtesy Library of Congress.*

maketh his son or his daughter to pass through the fire, [or] that useth divination [or] an observer of times, or an enchanter, or a witch, Or a charmer, or a consulter with familiar spirits, or a wizard, or a necromancer. For all that do these things [are] an abomination unto the LORD: and because of these abominations the LORD thy God doth drive them out from before thee." (Deuteronomy 18:10). Scientific skeptics and atheists generally feel religious rituals and secular séances to be scams.

The many variations of thought and faiths that do or do not believe in the practice is complex. Some psychics are new age, or even Christian, and almost all cultures, such as Native American, African (Voodoo) and others called upon ancestors for aid in perilous times. As mankind has sought answers to what life is about, he has feared what lies afterward and sought answers from those passing over the veil for solace. Sometimes they have disturbed spirits to divine for arcane knowledge, to find treasure or answers to any number of questions. Of course disturbing these souls was thought to be highly risky and so protection was used to help ensure the safety of the summoner. *Communicating with the Dead: Reach Beyond the Grave* by Jeff Belanger is a great book that looks into the history and practice of spiritual communication devices. It also covers scientists, clergy, and psychics who try make contact with the spirit world. Tarot Cards, which began as a card game, have evolved as a system that can be used for divination. Another divination tool is runes. Their users, known as runecasters, believe they are communicating directly with the gods. This has been around since prehistoric man first cast bones and is also practiced by Voodoo and Hoodoo priests. Gypsies at carnivals who told fortunes would stare into crystal balls to see into the spirit world.

Another form of divination, Necromancy, was performed by those referred to as Necromancers. The Necromancer wore clothing from corpses and ate tasteless foods, avoided women, and many other forms of denial of the self all in an attempt to connect with the dead and their energies, so deep was their determination to gain the secrets from the dead.

People, from Franciscan friar Roger Bacon to Dr. John Dee, adviser to Queen Elizabeth, sought out divination practices to connect with the spirits of the dead, as did Eliphas Levi in the 1800s. Freemasons and members of the Golden Dawn mentioned divination and spirit contact, and many modern writers have touched upon this taboo and misunderstood subject.

OUIJA BOARDS

Alistair Crowley

Ouija boards, boards marked with symbols, letters and numbers, have a variety of other names, such as spirit board or talking board. A movable indicator called a planchette, also known as an "eye," is moved about the board in attempts to get messages by communicating with spirits. The first-known board, used by the Greeks, was one used by the philosopher Pythagoras, in 540 B.C. His sect would conduct a séance using a devise on wheels that moved towards symbols, which he then interpreted to the audience as "being revelations supposedly from an unseen world."

The talking board, as we know them today, started as a novelty invented by Elijah Bond, an attorney, on February 10, 1891. By 1901, Bond started production of his own boards under the name Ouija, until a competitor, by the name of Fuld, contested Bond, claiming that he had invented it. In 1966, Fuld's estate sold his business to Parker Brothers, who continues to hold all trademarks and patents. A glow in the dark model was brought out as well.

The Modern Spiritualist Movement in the United States in the middle of the twentieth century used these boards so much that they created a trend which we attribute to the popularity of the Ouija board today.

Aleister Crowley, a British occultist, was fond of the Ouija board. He used one off and on, recommending it to his students saying, "Your Ouija board experiment is rather fun. You see how very satisfactory it is, but I believe things improve greatly with practice. I think you should keep to one angel, and make the magical preparations more elaborate."

These boards have become an iconic part of culture, appearing in many books and movies, from being just an object in and of itself, to an evil demon taking on the guise of a board. The 1971 novel *The Exorcist* by William Peter Blatty, and the 1973 movie based off of it, portrays the character Regan telling her mother that she has used an Ouija board to contact an entity calling itself Captain Howdy. Just prior to her possession by a demon, Regan demonstrates her contact with Captain Howdy but the planchette flies off the Ouija board.

On the July 25, 2007, edition of the paranormal radio show *Coast to Coast AM*, host George Noory attempted to carry out a live Ouija board experiment on national radio with guests, Dr. Bruce Goldberg (a renowned hypnotherapist), author Rosemary Ellen Guiley (a leading expert on the paranormal and supernatural) and Jerry Edward Cornelius (a Thelemic magician and follower of Aleister Crowley). In the time leading up to the show's airing, unfortunate events kept occurring to friends and guests, so Noory canceled the experiment.

Houdini séance, *Courtesy Library of Congress.*

SÉANCES

Séances have been held since the 1700s. The word *séance* comes from the French *séance*, meaning "seat" or "session," from Old French *seoir*, meaning "to sit." In English, however, the word came to be used more specifically for a meeting of people who desire to receive messages from or send them to those who have passed on. *Dialogues of the Dead*, published in England in the 1760s, was one of the earliest books on séances.

There have been several famous mediums, such as the two sisters, Kate and Margaret Fox, who were around in the mid 1800s. As youngsters these sisters lived in an old farmhouse, that was thought to be haunted, in Hydesville, New York. Frightened by mysterious knocking sounds, Kate asked the unknown source of the rapping to knock the same number of times as she snapped her fingers. She claimed that after she did so, her spectral visitor responded with the same number of sounds. Over a number of sessions, they developed a yes-or-no system and ultimately, using an alphabet knocking system, the girls claimed that they were conversing with a man that had been murdered in the house.

The town's residents heard of the phenomenon and the stir it caused helped create the legend of the girls' ability to have spiritual contact. Later, the girls moved to live with friends in Rochester and their reputation spread quickly among the Quakers. By the year 1850, the famous sisters began holding séances all over New York. Despite the Fox's admission later that the events had been staged, a good portion of the country remained convinced that mediums could actually communicate with the departed.

Mary Todd Lincoln, who, mourning the loss of her husband, President Abraham Lincoln, tried to contact him by organizing Spiritualist séances in the White House with other prominent members of society. The Spiritualist movement held its popularity despite an 1887 report that tried to expose it as fraud and showmanship. Other believers in Spiritualism included author of *Sherlock Holmes*, Arthur Conan Doyle, and the inventor of telephone, Alexander Graham Bell. Harry Houdini, who said he was not a disbeliever of Spiritualism itself, was incensed by the trickery of those he considered frauds. Spiritualism has seen its peaks during national wars, from the Civil War to our present day. People want answers, and are easily fooled because they seek hope in their times of sorrow.

The movie *The Haunting in Connecticut* portrayed both séances and ghosts at unrest. In this story, a young man dying of cancer contacts a minister, whom he met at the hospital, for help dealing with his paranormal experiences. The minister informs the boy that the visions and supernatural encounters are likely a result of the previous occupant's occult activities, séances, and necromancy conducted by the mortuary owner in the 1820s.

Although reported to be based on a true story experienced by the Snedeker family in the 1980s, this may not be the case. As the book's author, Ray Garton, said, "I never met the son, who was said to be ill, although I was allowed to talk to him on the phone once, supervised by Carmen, his mother. When the boy began to talk about drugs and told me that he didn't hear and see strange things in the house once he began taking medication, Carmen ended the conversation."

Ray Garton, in the book *In a Dark Place: The Haunting in Connecticut,* the story follows the fictional family, the Campbells, as they move into a house (a former mortuary) to mitigate the strains of travel on their cancer-stricken son, Matthew. The family soon becomes haunted by violent and traumatic events from supernatural forces occupying the house. Matthew is aided by Jonah (one of the spirits inhabiting the house), and eventually discovers the truth about the house's spirits. The story comes to a climactic resolution with the burning of the house and close escape of its residents. The family insists on its reality, as does Tim Yancy, a thirty-five year investigator into the paranormal who has assisted police. Mr. Yancy runs Encounters Paranormal Radio and has a reputation of investigating seriously violent hauntings. Mortuary equipment was discovered in the basement of the house, and the well-known paranormal expert Lorraine Warren commented, "In the master bedroom, there was a trap door where the coffins were brought up, and during the night, you would hear that chain hoist, as if a coffin were being brought up." The Warrens founded the New England Society for Psychic Research in 1952 and later opened the Occult Museum. Mrs. Warren's husband, Ed, is an author and together they have investigated several famous hauntings, most notably The Amityville House in New York, another home possessed by spirits yet riddled with controversy in its credibility. Despite stipulation as to the reality of the case, it is an extremely well -done movie, showing examples of what I have written about here, and I enjoyed the feature in the DVD, "Memento Mori: The History of Post Mortem Photography."

Stage Mediumship Séances

In the religion of Spiritualism, part of the religious services is the practice of communication with the dead. The leader, commonly called "a medium" would use a ritual whereby he would repeat what he believes are messages to the living participants who are seated around a table. The medium falls into a trance that then allows the spirit(s) to communicate through the medium by what is known as automatic writing, a series of raps, the floating of a table or any number of "supernatural" events. Sometimes, even today, this is done for entertainment.

Since séances are usually held in a circle in low light, it is easy for less ethical "mediums" to cheat, considering the participants are eager to contact a loved one. This has led to a general perception that all séances are faked or that all mediums are frauds. Despite this suspicion, a growing trend is on a new type of séance that has become popular, known as "stage mediumship séances," which takes place in front of an audience. Sylvia Brown and John Edward, who has gained considerable fame in shows like *Crossing Over with John Edward* and *John Edward Cross Country*, claim to relay messages and advice from audience members' relatives and loved ones who have passed on. Mr. Edward says he was convinced at a young age that he was able to communicate with the dead, and after writing his first book on the subject in 1998, he became a well-known but controversial figure in the United States through his shows broadcast on SCI-FI Channel beginning in July 2000.

Just as in the past, people have attempted to expose these mediums as frauds. Critics of Mr. Edward assert that he performs the mentalist techniques of hot reading and cold reading, which are techniques used by mentalists, fortune tellers, and con artists to ascertain details about another person, often in order to convince them that the reader knows much more about a subject than they actually do by analyzing the client's body language, age, ethnic or religious background, sexual preference or style of fashion. Cold readers commonly employ high probability guesses about the subject, quickly picking up on signals from their subjects as to whether their guesses are in the right direction or not, and then emphasizing and reinforcing any chance connections the subjects acknowledge while quickly moving on from missed guesses. Hot reading is the use of foreknowledge when giving answers to clients' questions through a variety of means, such as background research or overhearing a conversation. Hot reading is commonly used in conjunction with cold reading.

This is used by some television psychics in conjunction with cold reading, as can be seen on the comedy show *Psych*, on the USA Network, where the lead actor plays a con artist "psychic" private detective (James Roday) and has a reluctant sidekick named Gus, played by Dule Hill. Shaun, the "psychic," uses his shrewd observations to solve crimes for pay from local police. In this case, no harm is done, but unethical people have used such things for nefarious purposes as well. In these questionable cases, the psychics may have clients schedule their appearances ahead of time, and then collect information using collaborators like door -to -door salesmen, or religious solicitors, who then pass on the information to the psychic. The psychic will then place the person strategically in the audience. In 2001, a *Time* magazine article reported that psychic John Edward used this method on his television show, *Crossing Over*, where an audience member who received a reading was suspicious of prior behavior from Edward's aides. Allegedly, the show's workers began conversations with audience members and asked them to fill out cards detailing their family trees. His accuracy on television has been questioned by some due to the editing process of removing sections where it doesn't produce conclusions needed for the show. Edwards responds to these allegations by saying "People are in the studio for eight hours, and we have to edit the show for time, not content. We don't try to hide the misses." Still another source who saw a John Edward show in Pennsylvania advised that the only time staff came out was to tell them how long a wait there would be before he came on stage. There was no other interaction.

As my friend, psychic medium Reverend Tim Shaw, points out on hot and cold reading,

"Mediums, I think, all do ... because we are observers of the smallest things ... We listen more intensely to pick up the vibrations, and cold reading is something we are all aware of and try not to be affected by. I call that observations ... You need to admit if something that you physically see may be a part of the reading... By admitting the observation you gain trust and try to be as honest in the reading as possible. I leave it up to the reader to judge the belief or disbelief of any psychic's work."

He explains an example to me as follows,

"If I have a client sitting there wearing a shirt with a dog print on it ... and I am getting a message talking about a dog, what do I do? This way they know that I have seen the shirt and will bring the message through regardless. That is the mark of a good medium, humility."

As for the unethical mediums directly taking advantage he says,

"The problem comes in when people do this for their only income. Then they need to be flashy and get people to come back. Me—if you do or don't doesn't matter to me."

Séance photo fake, *Courtesy Library of Congress.*

The exposure of supposed mediums whose use of séance tools derived from these techniques (stage magic) has been disturbing to many believers in spirit communication. In particular, the 1870s exposure of the Davenport brothers as illusionists and the 1887 report of the Seybert Commission, brought an end to the first historic phase of Spiritualism. Stage magicians, such as John Neville Maskelyne and Harry Houdini, had a sideline hobby of exposing fraudulent mediums and protested during the late nineteenth and early twentieth centuries, in an attempt to expose fraud of tool-using mediums. Skeptics often point to historic exposures and all spirit mediumship as inherently fraudulent, while believers have tended to eliminate the use of tools but continued to practice mediumship in full confidence of its spiritual value to them. Some self-proclaimed mediums are fully conscious whereas others seem to be in a partial or full trance during their work. Trance-mediums usually say when they end their trance that they retain little or no recollection of the messages they received so they record them or have an assistant who writes down or otherwise records their words.

Channeling is a modern term for mediumship which is slightly different. Channeling is where the medium allows a spirit limited use their body to communicate with an audience.

Séance Tools and Techniques

During the latter half of the nineteenth century, a number of Spiritualist mediums began to advocate the use of specialized tools for conducting séances, particularly in leader-assisted sessions conducted in darkened rooms. Spirit slates consisted of two chalkboards bound together that, when opened, were said to reveal messages written by spirits. "Séance tables" were special light-weight tables which were said to rotate, float, or levitate when spirits were present. "Spirit cabinets" were portable closets into which mediums were placed, often bound with ropes, in order to prevent them from manipulating the various aforementioned tools. These cabinets could either be actual pieces of furniture or a corner of the room that was simply separated by a curtain. This was the medium's work space and it was said to be used to attract the spiritual forces. While some mediums seek to achieve larger financial success by conducting a séance standing alone before an audience, the traditional séance has always been conducted around a circular table.

Margery Crandon also became well known for supposed spiritual abilities at a time when the popularity of the craft was in decline due to the questioning of authenticity of many mediums. Much of her popularity came from her risqué habits, such as sometimes performing her séances in the nude and having affairs with her critics. During the time of her popularity, the magazine *Scientific American* offered $2,500 to anyone capable of convincing a panel of respected experts that there was no deception in her séances. One of the judges was Harry Houdini, renowned stage magician.

Spirit trumpet, photograph of item in the collection of Medium Reverend Timothy Shaw, Courtesy Rev. Shaw, 2010.

Spirit slates, photograph of item in the collection of Medium Reverend Timothy Shaw, *Courtesy Rev. Shaw, 2010.*

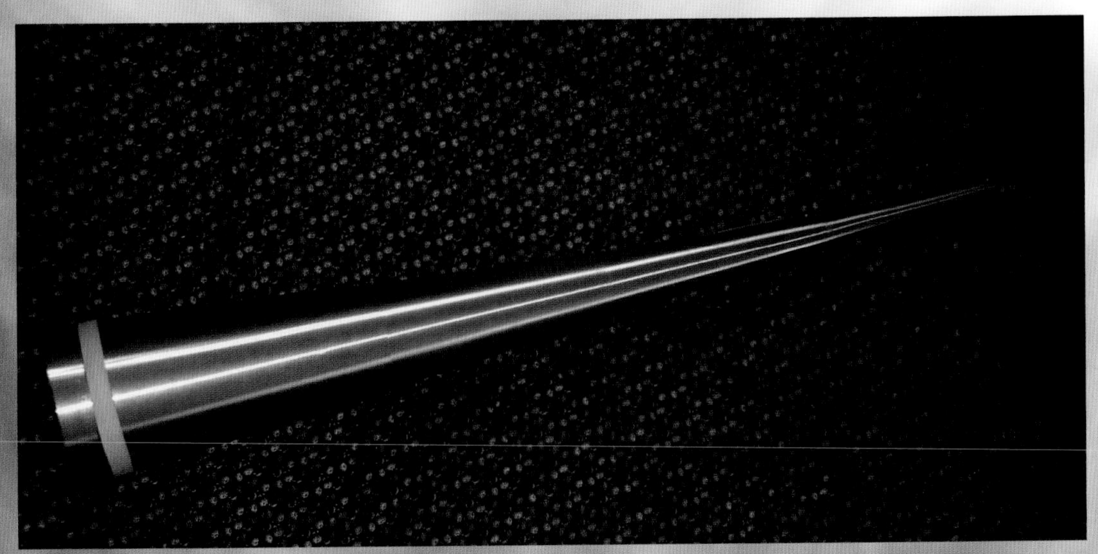

CHAPTER SIX

DEATH EMBRACED—GOTHIC CULTURE

"Life and Death are both lonely states of existence."

~ Kindra Ravenmoon

Few among us can handle the realities of life, with the inevitable one being our own demise. To face our own mortality is frightening. This is clearly evident through our fascination with horror novels from such authors as Stephen King and Dean Koontz, Gothic novels like Bram Stoker's *Dracula* and Mary Shelley's *Frankenstein*, and portrayals of popular anti-heroes in such films as *Batman, The Punisher, Death Wish, The Crow, Spawn, Pirates of the Caribbean*, and *Interview with the Vampire*, as well as countless others that depict good guys and girls with a hint of "evil" or bad-boy/girl qualities.

In the human psyche, we have an age-old fear of the unknown. Death is the ultimate unknowable no matter how science continues to progress. In the early twentieth century, Carl Jung developed a theory about something he called the "shadow," a term to describe the hidden fears, doubts, and irrational parts in the psyche we collectively share. He claimed this was the source of motivation and inspiration, which presents itself in the creations of art, poetry, and music. When we refuse to face our "shadow," it can present itself in ways we wish we could deny, from attitude problems, to a failure to cope with life because we repress our darkest emotions, *especially* those that may not be considered socially acceptable. Stereotyped by the mainstream, Goths are one of those subcultures born out of the desire or willingness to face their "shadow" without fear, and embrace their darker nature as well as triumphantly rise above its weight to be productive members of society.

Gothic fashion designer Kambriel,
Courtesy of Kambriel, 2010.

WHAT IS GOTH

Gothic model Kindra, *Courtesy model collection, 2009.*

What *is* Goth? This may be one of the most-often posed questions pertaining to this particular subculture, and the definition is elusive. Goth is actually much more than the sum of its parts, many of which are valid aspects of several other subcultures. It is more than a label, style, or description. Goth is both a lifestyle and a philosophy that has its roots firmly embedded in the historical past and our ever-changing present.

The central ideal that characterizes Goth is an almost compulsive drive toward creativity and self-expression, and a desire to reach out to an audience and share our deep fascination with all things frightening, odd, and mysterious. Goth can be either subtle and seducing or nightmarish and shocking, but it does play on what society secretly cannot acknowledge to itself about its own sense of duality.

As a lifestyle, Goth is as diverse as the people that inhabit its dark domain. There is no true unifying stereotype or dress code, but a certain dark taint is prevalent in the fashion that defines them. Not all Goths are depressed or employ the same modes of self-expression. This tends to create confusion over what Goth truly is, but this diversity is also one of its defining factors. The commonly held idea of Goth is that of the maladjusted, antisocial outcast who attempts suicide on a regular basis and is incredibly proud of the scars left from previous attempts. This idea is utterly false. While some Goths are outcasts and often feel depressed or alone, many are no more maladjusted, antisocial, or depressed than anyone else.

Goths deal with the same pressures that others do; the same stresses, social anxieties, family problems, etc. In choosing to express their angst, they also find themselves dealing with a great deal of rejection, intolerance, judgment, and prejudice. Charles Taylor, in his article entitled "Wild Children" on Salom.com says, "the people who have set themselves so firmly against Goth kids and all the other kids who don't conform have yet to grasp that the suffocating perfection they present is the best argument for the styles they're decrying."

Many people believe that Goths are obsessed with death when in actuality it is more a matter of acceptance and acknowledgment of the inevitable. This thought process challenges the way most traditionally think about such things. Gothic subculture has the advantage, for the most part, of a better grasp of understanding and coming to terms with the darker aspects of life, loss and death. With an of acceptance of the fate that awaits us all, rather than denying death, they instead accept it as a natural part of life, as a part of the natural balance of things.

THE HISTORY OF GOTH

The modern Goth movement has its roots in Western Europe and North America during the late 1970s and early 80s. This counter culture was, and still is, dominated by dissatisfied youth hailing from mostly middle-class structures. Children of highly restrictive families were left, unlike their parents, with a strong feeling of instability and lack of personal or group identity. Responding to the confusion and lack of personal identity, a few of the brightest and most creative children of these families began to create their own social structure based on a synthesis of historical elements, dramatic traditions, philosophies, and schools of thought such as those popular in Byronic England, along with most of Europe at that time, and the imagery of the Gothic and Romantic periods. Borrowing heavily from an earlier group of like-minded individuals, such as *Frankenstein,* author Mary Shelley and her friend, poet and scoundrel, Lord Byron of the Romantic Period, the New Romantic, or antiquity Goths evolved, as their counter-culture grew.

Goth soon split into two distinct types, one Apollonian and the other Dionysian in its approach, by the 1980s. The Apollonian faction concerned itself with the artistic and philosophical facets of the Goth subculture. For the most part, these people were fairly non-confrontational in their means of self-expression, being poets, artisans, or philosophers. They were typically obsessed with the act of creation and the appreciation of literature, art, and music, even if they themselves were not creating the works. Some attempts were made to legitimize this subculture in the eyes of its parent culture, but such acts met with very little success. Because they were regarded as harmless—morbid dreamers, if you will—these Goths were tolerated. The more Dionysian faction of the Goth subculture passionately embraced the most hedonistic and often more self-destructive facets of the movement. Their contributions were more ephemeral and less easy to define in traditional terms such as creativity, but they were still vibrant with the haunted, dark spirit of the counter-culture. Some of the more prominent Goth musicians and thinkers, musician and satirist, Voltaire, or filmmaker Tim Burton, belonged to this faction.

The modern stereotype of Goth is a twisted caricature of the more obvious appearance, making much of its decadence and tendency towards self-destruction more prominent while entirely missing its subtle artistry and depth that it truly started out with. By the 1990s, Goth had almost completely vanished, as members of the subculture were forced to accept conformity to ensure individual survival as adults. Like myself, and those marginal percentages of the original Goth community, some were able to adapt to adult life and yet remain essentially and visibly true to themselves.

By this time, the new generation of disaffected youth had already begun to imitate what they had perceived of the predecessors, or Elder Goths. These youth embraced the dark coloring and a superficial, and more emotionally driven, attitude of the previous Goth subculture combining it with the punk rock style of dress to become what are now called "Emo". "There is not only one type of Goth person that associates or identifies with the Gothic scene and thus, as with most groups, the stereotypes merely exaggerate some of the more common characteristics of those most visible to the public. Typically the most visible are the worst examples and Goths themselves often enjoy making fun of these stereotypes by mocking them," says John J. Coughlin, author and expert on Goth culture and witchcraft. An extensive list of Goth types are outlined in my work, *Embracing the Darkness; Understanding Dark Subcultures.*

Artistic Expression and Goth

The rebellious characteristics of the Goths have prevailed throughout time and are evident in many forms of expression. Milton's *Paradise Lost* as well as Dante's *Inferno* depict grotesque scenes of wildly cavorting demons and corpses, confusedly mixing elements of Paganism and Christian "Devil worship." The works of Edgar Allan Poe, who was likely influenced by eighteenth-century opposition to rigid social values, often delved into themes about man's psychotic nature and loss of inhibitions. Lord Byron was equally applauded and scorned for his erotic poetry and scandalous personal life. Such rebellion and decadence is the hallmark of the Romantic or Antiquity Goth.

I spoke some time ago to fashion designer Kambriel, who explained, in depth, her views on Goth, life, and fashion. The décor of dark culture is showcased and greatly influenced in modern culture trickling into fashion models, designs, and all black nail polish, significant in the fact that it was commonly stereotyped as a Goth look and avoided by outsiders. In recent years, styles like CyberGoth have come about and have pushed aside the "Antiquity Goths" in their popularity. CyberGoths express themselves with a futuristic flair, immediately recognizable by their glowing neon graphic accents on a stark backdrop of severe shapes, stemming from our entrance into the twenty-first century.

I believe there will always be a place for Romantic Goths and their styles and designs, which can still be seen at events such as Dracula's Ball in Philadelphia or the Vampire Balls of New York and New Orleans. Many wear black, whether it be as a symbol of aloofness, a rebellion against norms of society, or simply because it's sleek. A powerful color in fashion, black pays tribute to the classic horror genre; it represents contempt for a gray and stagnate world, or provides the ultimate contrast to an overly saturated and falsely cheerful facade. When not worn to simply copy a trend, it is a statement of subversion and a denial of constantly changing mainstream fashion trends. Black has a timeless appeal, perfectly balanced with the aspects of Gothic art and style.

The aspects of Goth in fashion, the coverings by which most of us are judged, have only slightly changed over the ages. It just so happens that those of us immersed in this type of lifestyle can clearly see "good" and "bad" aspects of life simply as normal life. Individuals who walk this less-traveled path may appear unable to fit into mainstream society.

Embracing the Darkness; Understanding Dark Subcultures Courtesy Dark Moon Press, 2009.

Amidst The Dead, graphic art by Drake Mefestta, *Courtesy Ticia Martyr Image Photography, 2010.*

Magic Meets Gothic

Dark spirituality is the embracing of the spiritual shadow, with all its truths exposed, baring our inner fears. Truth, like energy, is neither good nor bad, it simply *is.*

Society has trouble accepting people who are different than the accepted norm, and tends to reject any multi-theistic path or faith that focuses primarily on self-awareness. Currently, there is no generally accepted, single definition for the word "Pagan." This term is widely used by Atheists, Agnostics, Humanists, etc., to refer to themselves. It has come to describe a person who does not follow an Abrahamic religion.

One website (GodHatesGoths.com) is reported by those in the Gothic community to be an example of an exaggerated, fundamentalist Christian point of view. Presenting themselves as the official website of an organization "Parents Against Goth" headed by Rev. R. G. Green, research seems to show that no such organization or person exists. The site states:

> "Goths are proud of their sin, proud to parade around like sick Halloween freak-shows, proud to degrade their bodies with tattoos and piercings, proud to engage in filthy sexual perversions, and in that prideful state they cannot repent – you cannot repent of something you're proud of. Pride is one of the Seven Deadly Sins which are hated by God."

This may sound extreme, but many people agree with this thought and think that is what Goth culture is all about.

My friend, author Raven Digitalis, is a Goth and has written several books on Goth, as well as pagan religious practices, merging the two in works such as *Goth Craft*, where he explains that Goth is an aspect of the person's inner nature coming out, the balance between light and dark, day and night. Gothic Pagans pay homage to the often overlooked powers of darkness, which, in many cases, involves the shadow realm of death, the counter aspects of the day. The Dark Goddess is shown in myths as crones, wise old hags, the personification of war and various stages of blight on the earth, and is known by many names. Some of the names the Dark Goddess is known by are Kali, Huntress, and Diana. The Dark Gods are the Lords of the Dead, underworld figures such as Hades and Set. There are many Lunar Gods and Goddesses, each part of the world and each in their own place, none being more important than the other. Simply put, just calling on the Gods and Goddesses of the night are sufficient. The circle of life is a constant. So is the cycle of the moon and of day into night. Nocturnal Witches simply choose to observe what is normally overlooked. It is not a rejection of the light, but an acknowledgment of a needed balance.

John J. Coughlin, author of *Out of the Shadows*, tells me "I usually call it 'Dark Paganism' only since 'Gothic' tends to assume it is only an aspect of the Gothic Subculture. I usually define it as a form of Paganism aligned to a left-hand path. There is often a certain attraction to themes and images of darkness (Gothic imagery so to speak), but a Dark Pagan may not 'look' like a Goth. The defining factors are more in perception and attitude. Since I was always drawn to dark themes and imagery it was only natural for me to begin to incorporate such things into my personal developing spirituality. The idea of calling myself a Dark Pagan only came to me when I found it harder to define myself simply as 'Pagan' and found myself lacking a simple way to describe myself to others." While not all Goth are pagans, in fact there are Goths of every religion, the majority of those leaning toward a love for the macabre and who practice a non-Christian, Muslim or Jewish faith are much more likely to be.

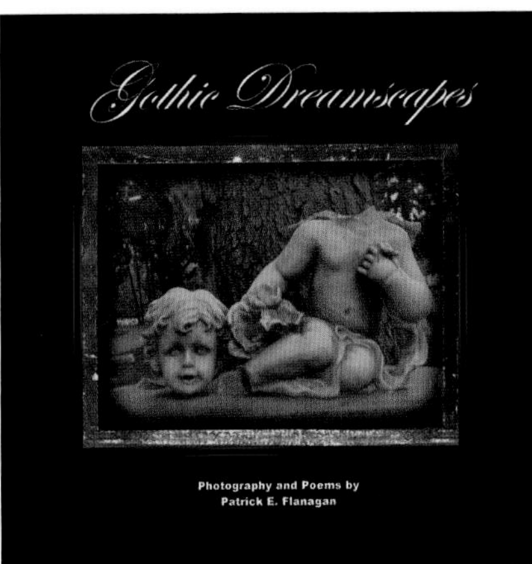

Gothic Dreamscapes by Patrick E Flanagan (Dark Moon Press). Poetry of a sombre nature for people who love cemeteries, showing that Gothic individuals are more mainstream than some may believe.

Opposite: Gothic-styled architecture of St. Andrews Church.

Death and Goth

Most people don't understand Goths and their fascination with frequenting cemeteries, but back in Victorian times people would go to cemeteries all the time, because they were not only resting places for the dead, but also beautiful parks.

A lot of Gothic art, literature, and music deal with death. But "Goths are not only these grim, somber creatures that the stereotypes always reflect," Nancy Kilpatrick says in her book, *The Goth Bible* (St. Martin's Griffin), "Many of these interests are things that society deems are macabre, but they are not macabre."

While the media tends to paint Goths as high-school-age kids with no ambitions in life, the majority I have met have jobs in fields such as music or art, web design, graphic design, computer programming, etc., and they simply leave the club clothes in the closet.

Though there may be many Goths who are of high-school age, there are also a lot of Goths who are older, in their 30s and beyond.

May Be Creepy ... But True

I found acceptance as I evolved out of the Romantic Goth style in favor for the suit and tie. I simply use what is known as the Corporate Goth style. This typically refers to, for me, an all black power suit, including shirt and tie, or sometimes dark shades of color such as burgundy, dark purples, scarlet, etc.

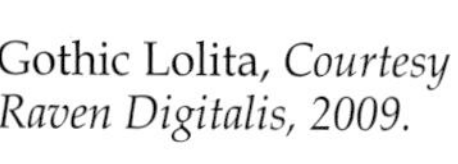

Gothic Lolita, *Courtesy Raven Digitalis, 2009.*

Alta Sin Whore Photo. *Courtesy of model Alta, 2009.*

Opposite:
Last Love, graphic art by Drake Mefestta, *Courtesy Ticia Martyr Image Photography, 2010.*

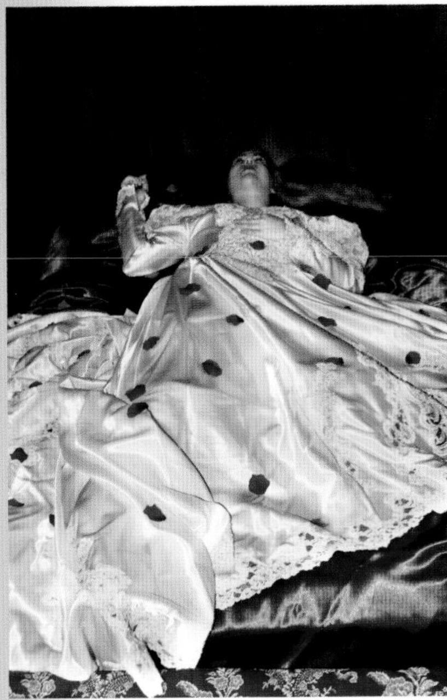

Above:
Deaths Bed, model Jess, *Courtesy Pendragon Studios Photography, 2009.*

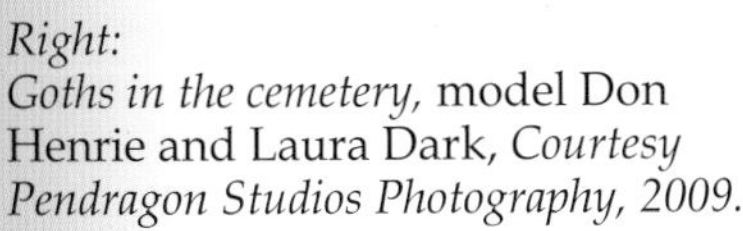

Right:
Goths in the cemetery, model Don Henrie and Laura Dark, *Courtesy Pendragon Studios Photography, 2009.*

Goth model Ivy Blue, *Courtesy Paul Erlandson, 2010.*

Opposite:
Gothic model Kindra,
Courtesy of model, 2010.

I am proud to call myself Gothique and most tend to view me as such putting me under the traditional gothic stereotyped category due to my style of dress, image and etc. ... That is fine but here is my definition of what true Goth really is: Gothique is a away a life and seeing the beauty in the macabre, admiring the somber beauty in death and props that represent death, to naturally have a dark nature and morbid sense of humor, to love and live the surroundings of an atypical lifestyle 24/7.

True gothic nature ***is not*** *trying to create some dark personality for oneself just as a fun fad or to look cool at Goth scene events, living a "normal" life usually and then on weekends or for certain events switching into vampire styled clothing pretending that you suck blood, behaving and talking in a different manner altogether. True Goth is not being in a constant state of depression, hating yourself, talking about your suicide plans and whining how you hate everything (one can be happy and be Goth). When one speaks of Gothic, the fashion and music associated with this term immediately pops into mind; this stereotype is not a bad thing, but I for one, like many others who term themselves as Gothic, are not all about clothing and accessories all the time and we do tend to dress in varied styles depending on taste and mood, and even though I love the classic Gothic music, artists, and styles of music normally falling under the Gothic umbrella, I also like many others, and am a huge metalhead. So next time you start to stereotype what true Goth is, remember that a Swedish Viking styled Death Metal dude can be a true Goth in nature, character and likes just the same as that pale raven haired waif dressed all in black is.*

True Goth is not to be afraid to be different as in being yourself and true to your will. It is not a fashion style/statement to impress or so called sub-culture of whiney introverts like most seem to see it or put themselves into. This pop-Goth, candy coated emo is not what I want to associate myself with.

Death is continuation within another form of existence; this can be seen as when the body ceases to function and completely shuts down due to either natural or unnatural circumstances and the mind continues existence within spirit or soul either reconnecting with the surrounding energies or preparing to be reborn into another shell in order to continue it's path of learning for one cannot learn everything needed for the individual soul in one mundane lifetime. One must experience several eras, come to know of various levels of science and correct mistakes made in order to progress towards and accomplish self-deification. Not every individual achieves this; many lives and deaths go wasted. These unfruitful souls become weaker and must work harder with every failed attempt of existence. Eventually such types become what we know as being truly dead, lifeless gray nothings floating helplessly between the veils of the realms within the mind's dimensions of the minds of the those who are progressing.

~ Kindra Ravenmoon, Goth Model

GOTH, DEATH AND THE ARTS

All of the various creative arts have made a strong emotional connection within the Gothic subculture, as they are all expressions of our deep emotions. I have made a great deal of friends and fans all over the world, both online and in my travels, and greatly enjoyed all of the wonderful works of every style imaginable.

One such influence on today's Goth scene, beginning in the early 1990s, can be found in the works of renowned artist and founder of Monolith Graphics, Joseph Vargo. Mr. Vargo began his artistic career by selling his artwork and wares at Renaissance Faires, and over the years Monolith Graphics has sold and distributed hundreds of thousands of prints and other pieces of merchandise featuring his original artwork to fans worldwide.

I quickly became friends with Joseph as we shared a love of the macabre, especially in art. When I asked him once what he thought was the appeal for people when it came to dark themes, old architecture, and Goth in general, he told me:

> *I realize that the subject matter of my art may not appeal to everyone, but there are a large number of people that find beauty in darkness. Overall, the whole Gothic era represents a very dark and mysterious period of civilization. Gothic architecture is one of the most ornate and artistic styles of design, and even though it originated in Medieval cathedrals, it has a very sinister connotation. Gargoyles were originally designed as wards against evil spirits, but this idea faded and was forgotten through the years while these foreboding monstrosities of stone endured the centuries. Castles represent mysterious places to explore, filled with dark secrets and ghosts, and graveyards are literally the domain of the dead, offering an eerily tranquil and serene escape from the world of the living.*

I asked musician, Drake Mefestta, whom I met years ago at Gothicfest in 2006, about his thoughts, as it related to him, on this subject when we met again in 2010. His introspection provides much insight for himself and others.

Serenade, Lady Rosetta Goth, model and musician. *Courtesy Pendragon Studios Photography, 2009.*

The concepts of death are as endless and as infinite as the understanding of existence itself and in this, fear of the unknown after the last breath is drawn can be correlated to the fear of death itself. Though there are countless points of view regarding the end or as some would see it, the beginning of life thereafter or life again in reincarnation, it can be agreed upon that the loss of life bears the tragedy of lost knowledge and wisdom carried by that departed individual. Often I have taken a walk through a cemetery, looked upon the seemingly countless headstones and thought of all the stories of unbelievable deeds, indescribable experiences, and lessons profound that the now deceased had when they lived, I will never have the chance to hear of any of them. This fact provokes a personal fear that I am sure many share, the fear of not completing all that we desire in life before our time has come to pass and/or the fear of being lost or forgotten in the sands of the ever-constant time.

With such a bleak and inevitable reality to face how can any good come of death? For beginnings, death can be seen as one of the greatest motivations humans can have. It inspires people to live richer and fuller lives while they are here; it inspires greater ambition to strive to make a significant mark upon the world lest we fade quietly and disappear. Death places greater significance on the value of life and all things encompassing there within, if not for the presence of death at all I believe we as a people would have made little progress in any aspect through the ages. Therefore I do not weep at funerals, particularly at ones in which I recognized the deceased had lived their lives fruitfully and were content with their accomplishments be them great or small. I celebrate the lives of the departed for I feel to do otherwise is a show that they were more of an object you wanted to hold on to forever instead of letting them go forth and progress. Of course it hurts to not have someone you care for around any further, but one cannot expect anything of this earth to be held onto forever. I believe this flesh is but a shell, a vessel to carry the essence through the age and then we shed it as the snake sheds its skin.

These Haunted Dreams, author Michelle Belanger, *Courtesy of Dark Moon Press, 2008.*

URN Gothic album art by author, *Scribings for a Forgotten Soul*, 2009.

So why does the Gothic sub-culture emulate and identify so much with death on its various levels? I have beheld many images of the morbid, macabre, and austere through my days and have created just as many of my own. I see the beauty in bereavement manifestations, the dark clothes, the even darker eye-makeup, and a classic pale face with obsidian hair because of a deep appreciation for the darker things in life. The appreciation comes from a natural desire to reflect the opposite of what is the light by giving the balance and illustrating the positive traits of the dark. Like death, the darker side of life many Goths portray outwardly in addition has a certain mystique and that alone holds a great attraction to many. Many Goths will also gravitate to the portrayal of the vampire, the fundamental symbol of defiance against death. In the interpretation the Gothic sub-culture adopts in the vampire, they portray an image of our wants and desire to have eternal youth and thereby enable the endless possibilities that death would take away. Whatever the reason, there is a unified appreciation of the darker side of life, which incorporates greatly the aspects of death, and the mystery and power of its influences in all cultures whether it is acknowledged consciously and comprehended or not.

~ Drake Mefestta

Drake Mefestta, musician and graphic artist, *Courtesy Ticia Martyr Image Photography, 2010.*

Gothic Beauty, artwork by author, 2004.

Shophistigoth, *Courtesy Raven Digitalis, 2009.*

Drake's music may not be as widely known as others, popular Goth bands *Bauhaus, Siouxsie and the Banshees, the Sisters of Mercy, Dead Can Dance*, but all of them share qualities. Many others have long been writing about death, from somber reflections in modern groups like *Evanescence*, to tongue-in-cheek works by comedian-performer Voltaire. Others, such as Type O Negative, did morbid to near tongue-in-cheek humor. Type O Negative frontman, Peter Steele, had a macabre sense of humor up until his early death on April 14th, 2010.

Type O Negative achieved cult status and was loved by fans around the world. The band's most recent label, SPV/Steamhammer Records, issued an online statement about Peter Steele's death. "It's with great sadness that we give our condolences to the family and friends of Peter Steele," it read. Almost stereotypically, Steele reportedly suffered from clinical depression, and he often reflected this mood in the band's doom-laden lyrics, dark image, and an often morbid sense of humor. Ironically, Type O released seven studio albums, with their most recent being 2007's *Dead Again*.

I'd like to leave you to contemplate a friend's writing on the subject of death in the introspection, that I think summarizes most of this sub-culture.

Spectral Hauntings, Courtesy Dark Moon Press 2010.

Ticia Agne Martyr, *Courtesy Ticia Martyr Image Photography, 2010.*

I myself embrace death for many reasons and respect the nature of our souls leaving our physical bodies when the time is right. I am one who is weary of the thought of death, but not so much for how I go, but what comes after. Though I believe there is something beyond my time on this earth in this lifetime, I am also open the other endless possibilities, so I choose not to worry much about such things. I just want to make sure my time on this earth is not wasted and no opportunity is overlooked. I want as much knowledge as possible and to live life to it's fullest. I choose to embrace the dark side of life because I find it beautifully enchanting and I seek that kind of knowledge. In my opinion the human race is obsessed with anything they don't have much knowledge on and with things they cannot have.

I think that our sub-culture encompasses the aspect of death to prepare and to understand; to not have fear, whereas others take on religions to help them through their fear of death. Most need the assurance of acceptance and pearly white gates to help them cope. I am in no way saying religion is bad whether you are Christian, Buddhist, Pagan or of the Church of Satan. In my opinion what you believe truly is what comes to you. I just believe some embrace it and others fear it.

In a way I think my view on death brings me more into the light of the reality on the subject. I'm preparing myself, and welcoming it when my time is right. However I also fantasize about it. I meditate in preparation for my time, and in that way I fade away from the reality of our present world and it can be hard to bring myself back. But my on going realization of it I feel benefits me rather than not. Death has a haunting melody that I could dance to for all time.

On the side of the coin there is fact of us losing a loved one. Having funerals to remember the life of ones lost is a celebration used all over the world since the beginning. But I celebrate ones time to leave here instead of feeling sorry for myself that they are gone. Don't get me wrong, mourning someone isn't wrong, but for those who get depressed or end their own life over something in that nature I find selfish. Death is a way to go on and leave your legacy behind, no matter what you decide to make it. When one dwells on the fear of death it consumes their lives instead of living life to its fullest with keeping in mind that your true intent is with you always and as long as that is pure than you can't steer wrong. Wasted time is a wasted in life and there is no time for that… You may as well just be… DEAD.

~ Ticia Agne Martyr

AFTERWORD

Death, feared as the most awful of evils, is really nothing. For so long as we are, death has not come, and when it has come we are not.

~ Epicurus

As I wrote this book I drew upon not only my love for history and the macabre wonders of Gothic culture, but also for a deeper and broader understanding of my fellow man from all walks of life. When a death separates us from loved ones, we grieve for the loss of the human companionship and interactions with friends and family we shared with them while they lived. I read somewhere once that when death occurs, we can no longer reach out and touch people; we experience the deep and very personal heartache from being separated from their physical beings, no longer having opportunities to share our joys and sorrows, to hear their laughter. A powerful thought to put your daily life into the proper perspective isn't it?

Through our limited existence on this planet we face the fact that life hangs in the balance of our daily events, and we all deal with it in differing ways. At times death is quick, from accidents, crime, and warfare. Although logic tells us we all must one day perish, how we cope with such a profound loss, as that from death, is very personal. How we face up to and deal with our grief is very individual. Some of us weep openly, still others take it in stride, stoically, feeling that when it comes time, they will silently grieve while being the source of strength for others they care for to carry on. It is a harsh and sobering reality made obvious in films like *My Sister's Keeper*. When I watched this I discovered, all the more, how precious life truly is. One sister was created to be spare tissue and organs for her sibling. The pain each felt in being so entwined in the fragility of each other, the death of the older one's cancer ridden boyfriend and the suffering of the family made me realize that people everywhere face the prospect of death not only as people grow old and leave us behind but at anytime.

I lost my family slowly over the years, and my favorite dog, Buddy, to whom I felt closer to than even some friends. Some of my best friends came close to, or did, lose people dear to them while I was writing this work. I think about how truly precious we are to one another, those family and friends we choose to live amongst each day. One can't help but feel we deprive ourselves moments we will never get back due to useless anger or time wasted being upset at trivial things, when living life to the fullest is so much more important.

Spend time with your friends and family. Cherish the pets you have and treat them well because one day you will not see them and you may have to face the next day feeling you could have and didn't. You can never take back time and replace it with a new day but you can make the next day better than the last. Strive to achieve happiness, success and do something that matters to you with your life. Don't live looking back saying I wish I had done something else. The movie *Last Holiday* had an impact on me where I came to see what such a simple grasp on taking charge of your life might truly lead to; a happier rest of our lives.

I wanted to learn and share this common tie we have called life and death, and further show, despite our varying religious traditions around the world, that through time, humanity's reverence for life will always be universal. While the sands of time never stop flowing through the hourglass, understand that it is up to you, as an individual, to see what is important around you. You, and only you, have ever had the power to shape the way the world will look back on you and remember you.

For myself, I write and create works of art while others leave their legacy in the minds of others through heroic sacrifices in dedication to duty to one's county, faith or in the very genetic offspring they leave behind, and other ways. Take a moment and think about the things and people that matter most to you, and how you would really want to be remembered. Perhaps if this work does nothing else beyond entertain and educate, as we all must walk into the arms of the Reaper eventually, I truly hope, for at least some, it may make you reflect on your own sense of value in the course of your existence.

About the Author

Occult researcher and Gothic fantasy artist E. R. Vernor, best known to his fans under the pen name Corvis Nocturnum, has owned an occult shop for several years while he maintained an office as the Vice President of the Fort Wayne Pagan Alliance, a faith tolerance organization, and acted as Vendor Director/Coordinator for Pagan Pride Day in Fort Wayne, Indiana. He has done lectures at various events all over Indiana, Ohio, and Illinois on the subjects in his first book *Embracing the Darkness; Understanding Dark Subcultures,* which details the truth and crossover of alternative lifestyles, gaining the attention of readers all over the world.

The grand and great-grandson of a Mason, he remains involved in bringing about public awareness to Goth culture, witchcraft, and Satanism's true nature at conventions and universities, by being an invited speaker at the 2006 World Religions Seminar at the Indiana-Purdue University Fort Wayne, and the guest panelist for the 2010 Kheperu Open House where he enlightened the convention attendees the misconceptions on Satanism. He has also been a consultant for A& E's *Paranormal States* episode *Satan's Soldier*. An active voice in many dark communities, Nocturnum has promoted public awareness on various issues, such as ethics, and explaining away stereotypes as host of his own radio show, *Embrace the Dark* and as a guest of a multitude of online radio shows. The author has had appearances in magazines such as the October 2009 *Penthouse* Magazine article interview on sex and Satanism, and he occasionally is a writer for *Dark Resurrected Magazine*.

Corvis Nocturnum/E.R. Vernor is a May 2010 graduate with Presidents List Honor Roll from Brown Mackie College, with dual associates degrees in Business Management and Criminal Justice. In his free time he enjoys oil painting works of fantasy, pagan, and Gothic artwork. He is the co-founder and publisher of Dark Moon Press.

Corvis Nocturnum can be reached for questions and appearances at: corvisnocturnum@yahoo.com or to written mail via P.O. Box 11496, Fort Wayne, IN 46858.

Other works by author include:

- *Embracing the Darkness; Understanding Dark Subcultures,* (Dark Moon, 2005)
- *A Mirror Darkly,* (Dark Moon Press, 2006)
- *Promethean Flame,* (Dark Moon Press, 2008)
- *Allure of the Vampire; Our Sexual Attraction to the Undead,* (Dark Moon Press, 2009)